Frank Sinatra

CELEBRITIES
Series Editor: Anthony Elliott

Published
Ellis Cashmore, *Beckham*
Charles Lemert, *Muhammad Ali*
Chris Rojek, *Frank Sinatra*

Forthcoming
Dennis Altman, *Gore Vidal*
Ellis Cashmore, *Mike Tyson*
Cynthia Fuchs, *Eminem*
Richard Middleton, *John Lennon*
Daphne Read, *Oprah Winfrey*
Nick Stevenson, *David Bowie*
Jason Toynbee, *Bob Marley*

Frank Sinatra

Chris Rojek

polity

First published in 2004 by Polity Press Ltd.

Polity Press
65 Bridge Street
Cambridge CB2 1UR, UK

Polity Press
350 Main Street
Malden, MA 02148, USA

ISBN: 0-7456-3090-1
ISBN: 0-7456-3091-X (pb)

A catalogue record for this book is available from the British Library and has been applied for from the Library of Congress.

Typeset in 11 on 13 pt Palatino
by Kolam Information Services Pvt. Ltd., Pondicherry, India
Printed and bound in Great Britain by MPG Books, Bodmin, Cornwall

For further information on Polity, visit our website: www.polity.co.uk

In Loving Memory of Keith Horner
(1953–2003)

It's Frank's world. We're just lucky enough to be able
to live in it.

Dean Martin

Look, make no mistake about it. Sinatra's a thug. Let's face it.
Let's be aware of it and let's try to use him to our advantage.

John F. Kennedy

You gotta love livin' because dyin' is a pain in the ass.

Frank Sinatra and Rat Pack motto

Hollywood is just full of guys waiting to be used. All anybody
there cares about is whether they're gonna be a star or not. We
help 'em along and we own 'em. That's how simple it is. And
the broads . . . beautiful and dumb. Shit, don't ever be star-struck
by all that movie baloney . . . they're all worthless bums and
whores. Hollywood is the only place I've ever been, besides
Washington D.C., where everybody – men and women – are just
beggin' for you to use 'em.

Sam Giancana, Chicago mobster

When I sing I believe I'm honest.

Sinatra, *Playboy* interview (1963)

CONTENTS

Preface   viii

INTRODUCTION   1

1 FRANK'S WORLD   7

2 *UOMO DI RISPETTO*   60

3 ANTINOMIES OF ACHIEVED CELEBRITY   96

4 THE RAT PACK   121

5 ENVOI   161

Notes   180

References   184

Index   187

PREFACE

The magical sleight of hand that makes a record like *My Way* become an anthem for Our Way is probably beyond our powers to fully understand at this stage in the development of scientific knowledge about human affairs. Why should the corny, bluff sentiments expressed by an ageing multimillionaire celebrity bruiser, a man who was frequently coarse, foul-mouthed and odious in his opinions, and was known to perpetuate friendships and business links with the Mafia, translate into the grace note of an entire generation and one of the prime symbols of an epoch? Doubtless, it is a matter of many factors: the quality of the music, the resonance of the sentiments with the spirit of the time, the commercial promotion of the music, the balance of power between age groups and the sexes, and so on and so forth. Yet the incontrovertible fact that Sinatra's music did this not once, but countless times in a career that stretched for nearly six decades also points to the unique contribution of the performer. Star quality may be a matter of many factors, but it flourished in the long career of Francis Albert Sinatra.

My generation, formed in the 1970s and 1980s, between the first OPEC oil crisis and the election of Ronald Reagan in the US and Margaret Thatcher in Britain, regarded Sinatra as a tainted period piece. We thought of him as a political reactionary, a friend of the disgraced former President Richard Nixon and his duplicitous Vice President Spiro T. Agnew, a *passé* superstar who uncomfortably tried to remain hip and relevant when the times had transparently left him becalmed in an entertainment world where the tuxedo and casino formed the essential accoutrements of performance. Who needed Frank Sinatra when we had Bob Dylan, the Beatles, the Rolling Stones, David Bowie, Roxy Music, the Sex Pistols and The Clash? The informality and directness of these performers rendered Sinatra's style of vocal delivery too mannered and objectionably fatherly.

So when Professor Anthony Elliott suggested that I consider writing a book for his Celebrities series with Polity, and mentioned Sinatra, Marlon Brando and Jack Nicholson as contenders, Sinatra was last on my list. Yet to revert to a propositional homily for the nonce, prejudice must never be permitted to dictate research. It was not long before my preparatory investigations into the careers and cultural impact of all three celebrities convinced me that Sinatra's achievements were far more diverse and impressive, and his public impact was deeper and likely to be more durable. With Sinatra we are dealing with that rare item in the firmament of achieved celebrity: a celebrity icon.

Moreover, I soon formed the additional opinion that there were tragic elements in Sinatra's stardom. In the studio-posed photographs from the early 1940s of the slender, callow-faced singer with the Harry James Orchestra and the Tommy Dorsey Band I saw something ineffably calculating and ruthless. It was as if the face of the young man betrayed signs of the pupae of pride and venality. The poet W. H. Auden famously described his own face as a "wedding cake left out in the rain." The studio shots of the young Sinatra displayed a carefully composed fresh-faced fawn that concealed a stiletto.

Because I am old-fashioned enough to believe that a proposition can only be confirmed through the process of *testing,* I tried out the idea of writing a book on Sinatra with my students. To my surprise, Sinatra was a more vital, considerable cultural presence to them than he had been to me when I was their age. If I may summarize their views: his music is classy, his films are often cool and funny (*The Manchurian Candidate* was celebrated as a prescient masterwork and *Ocean's Eleven* was acknowledged as the whacky original for George Clooney's popular remake) and, above all, he is a powerful symbol of masculine authority. While my students were somewhat aware of his relations with organized crime and his reputation for sexism and violence, they responded positively to the starkly unambiguous masculine image that he represented. It occurred to me that in an age rightly sensitive to the politics of difference, part of Sinatra's appeal to the young was his uncompromising *individualism*. The public face of Sinatra was of a man who possessed authority, acted decisively and was unapologetic about his success.

My first thanks then, must go to my undergraduate and postgraduate students in the Department of English, Media and Communication at Nottingham Trent University, and to Anthony Elliott, because without them the book would never have been written. My friendship with Roger Bromley and John Tomlinson in Nottingham Trent has been a crucial support to the book. The Institute of Cultural Analysis at Nottingham constitutes an imaginative and exciting research innovation and I consider myself fortunate to be part of it.

In addition, I am grateful to the person who more than anyone else fostered my sociological imagination: Eric Dunning. As Eric's student for nigh on four years in the 1970s at Leicester University, I never suspected I was under the tutelage of a Jekyll and Hyde. Since working in the East Midlands after 1996, I have much enjoyed Eric's late-night hospitality in Clarendon Park Road, Leicester. More to the point, I have discovered that beneath the public face of a passionate sociologist thrives a jazz addict and connoisseur. He has taught me much about Sinatra, to say nothing of the finer points of the music of Chet Baker, Dave Brubeck and Paul Desmond. In modest return, in February of 2002 I introduced Eric to one of Sinatra's most atmospheric drinking haunts, Tony's Bar on Mulberry Street, Manhattan. I also benefited from conversations with Alan Bryman, David Frisby, Gavin MacFadyen, Jim McGuigan, Gerry Peacock, George Ritzer, Christopher Simpson, Barry Smart and Bryan Turner. I am again indebted to Ann Bone, copy-editor *nonpareil*.

The FBI has released 2,403 pages of files pertaining to Sinatra on the internet under the Freedom of Information Act. This is an invaluable resource for anyone interested in Sinatra. It was essential to me in constructing a picture of his involvement with the Mafia. If you are interested in reading this material, the website is http://foia.fbi.gov/sinatra.htm. The transcripts of secretly taped FBI recordings of conversations relating to Sinatra reproduced in the book between Sam Giancana, Johnny Roselli, Johnny Formosa and other members of the Mafia come from this source. The material on the Castellammarese wars was assembled from interviews in New York, web research and a variety of crime encyclopedias. For a young Italian-American who was the occasional victim of racial abuse, like Sinatra in the 1930s, the Castellammarese wars provided a powerful role model of Italian-American cool and power. They certainly influenced Sinatra.

Shawn Levy's book on the Rat Pack (1998) and Nick Tosches' book on Dean Martin (1992) are standard works in the field and they provided the immediate intellectual context for my own research. I have now watched many DVDs and videos of Sinatra and listened to nearly all of his recordings. Belatedly, I now recognize that he was not only a magnetic celebrity icon of postwar culture, revealing many of the tensions of desire, deception and manipulation in the politics of fame, but a great artist.

INTRODUCTION

Why do celebrities matter? One way of responding to the question is to answer that they don't. According to this view, fame is a form of gross personality inflation, conjured up by the media and multinational corporations in the entertainment industry to win ratings wars and make money. But this places contestants in reality TV shows like *Big Brother* and *Survivor* on the same footing as Charlie Chaplin, Greta Garbo, Johnny Depp or Al Pacino. Audiences clearly differentiate between *types* of celebrity and can tell a celetoid (a one-minute wonder) from a person of enduring fame.

This begs the question of why some celebrities achieve enduring fame. Oddly overlooked factors here are *talent* and *persistence*. Those commentators who highlight the roles of media inflation and multinational financial manipulation are often the last to appreciate the talent and persistence that enduring celebrities possess. Of course, this is not to deny that celebrities are in fundamental ways *constructed* for us. A long chain of cultural intermediaries, consisting of personal managers, public relations staff, stylists, and image-makers, link enduring celebrities to the public. They are responsible for building and rebuilding the public face of the celebrity in transaction with the actions of the celebrity, the perceptions of the media, and the requirements of the audience. However, the emergence of *iconic* celebrities is never simply a matter of the wily, well-oiled stratagems of cultural intermediaries. Iconic celebrities are individuals who are positioned to imprint their personality upon an era. This is the result of the public recognition of unique talent or the special qualities of historical-cultural representation that the celebrity denotes.

Frank Sinatra was an iconic celebrity of the twentieth century. Even people who disapproved of his bravura lifestyle and outspoken opinions recognized his star power. In an extraordinary span lasting for 30 years between the early 1940s and his first, bogus retirement in 1971, Sinatra produced material that indelibly shaped the popular vernacular for dealing with love, loss, ageing, heartbreak, camaraderie, and ecstasy. When Sinatra first sang *All or Nothing at All, I'm a Fool to Want You, I've Got You Under My Skin, Angel Eyes, Night and Day, Come Fly with Me,* and *My Way,* he appeared to phrase emotions that were otherwise passionately mute or inchoate in the hearts of his audience. Before the elaboration of niche markets in popular music, with all of their many labels and layers of inclusion and exclusion, Sinatra appeared to sing for everyone. Later, as he grew into the role of 24-carat legend in postwar popular culture, the songs acted as an immediate gateway to nostalgia.

Yet from the outset, Sinatra's fame rested upon more than an alluring bel canto style of singing and superbly polished vocal phrasing. Pop icons differ from other celebrities in appearing to speak for their generation. They provide a sexual focus and a populist articulation of generational beliefs and values which lifts them from the confines of popular entertainment and bestows upon them general *cultural* and *political* significance. Sinatra rose to national and international prominence during the traumatic war years in the early 1940s. At this time, the big band domination of popular music made extensive use of sexually appealing male and female lead vocalists. Sinatra's position as the lead vocalist in first the Harry James Orchestra, and later the Tommy Dorsey Band, which in a typical swaggering aside he described as "the General Motors of the band business" (Levinson 1999: 78), seared his image in the public mind as a symbol for lost youth. This ensemble style of performance required the lead vocalist to be a member of a company, usually consisting of older men, and diffused public attention between many players. Sinatra's remarkable decision to go solo in 1942 reversed this balance of power. As a matter of course, he was gracious and solicitous about the musicians that accompanied him, but henceforward they would always be *his* backing band. Even in the artistically exhilarating concerts with Count Basie in the 1960s, Sinatra dominates.

A crucial aspect in his decision to go solo was the sexual candor of his new image. Sinatra professed to be bemused by the female hysteria that his incipient solo career generated. However, he also carefully cultivated his image as a sexually blessed Lothario. Al Jolson and Bing Crosby preceded Sinatra as iconic popular singers. But Sinatra qualifies for the accolade of being the original pop icon because he used his position at the zenith of youth culture in the 1940s to venture pronouncements on politics, class oppression, racial intolerance, and justice. Because of the controversy and notoriety that attached themselves like barnacles to Sinatra's public image after the late 1940s, it is easy to forget that during the war years and in their immediate aftermath, he appeared to many young Americans to be a veritable Richard the Lionheart, albeit Hoboken born, and with shady links to the heart of organized crime.

The hope that Sinatra expressed at this time, combined with his growing notoriety as an epic Lothario, incensed the moralistic media. Sinatra's wealth, sexual appeal, and political outspokenness was seized upon by virulent sections in the tabloid press who subjected him to disgraceful smear campaigns and vilification. The media which had fallen over themselves in their haste to elevate Sinatra to stardom, now sought to smite him. After 1947 Sinatra entered a career slump that was only reversed with his Oscar-winning performance in *From Here to Eternity* (1953), and the historically momentous recordings with Capitol in the 1950s. In these bitter, hard years, Sinatra was divorced by his wife, humiliatingly released from his Columbia Records contract, and summarily expelled from his exclusive MGM film contract. As younger performers succeeded him, he witnessed the eclipse of his fame as the unchallenged mouthpiece for youth. He descended to the precipice of career disintegration. Sinatra was badly treated by some sections of the media but, as he later acknowledged, he also acted as the architect of his decline. His hubris in the face of public allegations of

3

philandering and links with organized crime, and his carefree belligerence egged on the media critics. As he became more desperate to win back public acclaim he permitted himself to agree with advisors to take poor film roles and produce novelty recordings that deflated his hauteur.

The triumphant reversal of this nadir after 1953 became a career-long vindication of Sinatra's toughness and heroism. Sinatra felt blooded by his ordeal. The success that he enjoyed after 1953, along so many fronts, left him with an ill-judged feeling of invulnerability. The sexual shenanigans of the Rat Pack years, the highly public arguments with Capitol Records that eventually led to him breaking acrimoniously with the company, and his friendships and business relationships with executive members of the Mafia, were conducted with nonchalance. Sinatra grew so accustomed to living in the hiatus between public license and unpunished private caprice that he felt as if nothing could touch him.

What else can explain his disastrous decision in 1963 to permit a known Mafia chieftain, the notorious Sam Giancana, to stay at Sinatra's casino hotel, the Cal-Neva Lodge, Lake Tahoe, in direct violation of Nevada Gaming Control Board rulings? Giancana's visit was secretly filmed and culminated in Sinatra being divested of his gaming license. This, together with a wounding sense of grievance at being slighted by John F. Kennedy, for whom he had campaigned in the presidential election, tempered Sinatra's hubris.

In the early 1970s he changed his political spots. He campaigned for Richard Nixon in 1972, and befriended Nixon's unsavory running mate, Spiro T. Agnew. When Agnew was forced to resign the vice presidency in October 1973 after he had been revealed to be taking bribes from contractors in Maryland since 1967, Sinatra's defense lawyer, Mickey Rudin, took on the defense brief. Later in the decade, Sinatra became a fundraiser for Ronald Reagan. After defeating Jimmy Carter in the race to the White House, Reagan's effusive letter of support to the authorities was instrumental in Sinatra regaining his Nevada gaming license. Sinatra extended his charity work in this period. He also married Barbara Marx in 1976 and reports of the libertinism that had surrounded him throughout his life as a celebrity diminished. He maintained a punishing schedule of national and international concert tours. As his health deteriorated in the early 1990s, he often appeared to his public not so much as a legend but as a frail, and occasionally harrowing, living relic.

Sinatra's willingness to take risks, his passionate nature and his stoicism were celebrated as American virtues. The violence in his character was held to belong to the same frontier spirit of boldness that made America great. His multiple success as a recording artist, a film star and a record company executive confirmed the American dream. His whimsical generosity and practice of high tipping endeared him to the ordinary people from whose ranks he sprang. All of this was permitted to eclipse Sinatra's known Mafia connections and the abrasive, intimidating traits that often surfaced in his personality.

The last decade and a half has witnessed a remarkable renaissance of interest in Sinatra and the Rat Pack. It began with Quentin Tarantino's film *Reservoir Dogs* (1992), in which the protagonists are dressed in suits and ties that echo the Las Vegas Rat Pack look of the 1950s. The involvement of younger rock idols like Bono in Sinatra's final *Duets* recordings helped to legitimate Sinatra in modern youth culture. More recently Stephen Soderbergh's remake of *Ocean's Eleven* (2001), with George Clooney in the lead role played by Sinatra in the original version of the film, and Robbie Williams's release of his homage to Sinatra, *Swing When You're Winning* (2001), and a live tribute album, *Live at the Albert Hall* (2001), have added to the process.

In part, this development should be interpreted as a nostalgic *recherche du temps perdu* in contemporary popular culture. It looks back to an age of American global ascendancy, an age when American ideology presented the nation as the friend of the oppressed and the foe of the oppressor; and where celebrities appeared to be unvarnished, sexually unambiguous, and cool – an age indeed, before 9/11. Sinatra and the Rat Pack transmitted a generally benign view of masculine domination, a consistently but, for the day, socially acceptable sexist set of attitudes toward women, and a serene introspection in relation to global politics. The public face they concocted of carefree existence, guiltless priapism, easy success, immense wealth, and physical well-being provided a template of cool living. Among American postwar myths in popular entertainment, it is one of the most potent and enduring. While academics write reams on class, white power, and patriarchy, they often ignore the direct influence of powerful figures in the entertainment industry to act as role models or sources of fantasy in the lives of ordinary people. It is tempting to analyze these figures as expressions of the interests of abstractions like "the culture industry" or "the dominant class." But it is also shallow to do so. Achieved celebrity icons are seldom the pawns of obscure power blocs. They embody complex and contradictory relations with society, articulating images of belonging, recognition, identity, and resistance. In studying Sinatra we may hope to gain insights into how the process of achieved celebrity combines and correlates myth, individual experience and the specifics of individual psychology with nothing less than the course of collective history.

one

FRANK'S WORLD

Frank Sinatra was a World War One baby, born in 1915.[1]
He became a popular music phenomenon during the Second
World War. By his own account, audiences adopted and idol-
ized him then not merely as an innovative and accomplished
vocalist – his first popular sobriquet was "the Voice" – but also
as an appealing symbolic surrogate for American troops fighting
abroad. In the late 1940s his career suffered a precipitous decline. There were four reasons for this.

First, the public perception of Sinatra as a family man devoted
to his wife, Nancy, and their children, Nancy, Frank Jr and Tina,
was tarnished by his high-octane affair with the film star Ava
Gardner. The public face of callow charm and steadfast moral
virtue that Sinatra and his publicist George Evans concocted
during his elevation to celebrity was damaged by his admitted
adultery. Sinatra's reputation for possessing a violent temper –
he punched the gossip columnist Lee Mortimer at Ciro's nightclub[2] and took to throwing tantrums and hurling abuse at other
reporters when the line of questioning took a turn he disapproved of – became a public issue at this time.

Second, servicemen were understandably resentful of Sinatra's celebrity status. They regarded it as having been easily
achieved while they fought, and their comrades died, overseas.
Some members of the media stirred the pot by insinuating that
Sinatra pulled strings to avoid the draft. During the war, like
most entertainers, Sinatra made a virtue of his patriotism in his
stage act and music/film output. For example, his film *The
House I Live In* (1945), which won a special Academy Award in

1946, was a short, ten-minute paean to racial tolerance and the virtues of civic harmony. Devised by Sinatra and the director Mervyn LeRoy, the film aimed to present a vision of American society cleansed of domestic bigotry and violence. In a key scene Sinatra, only 30 years old at the time, provides a rousing homily to a group of antisocial, dysfunctional boys on the evils of prejudice which would have been enough to make Abraham Lincoln weep:

> Look fellas, religion makes no difference except maybe to a Nazi or somebody stupid. Why, people all over the world worship God in many different ways. God created everybody. He didn't create one people better than another... This wonderful country is made up of a hundred different kinds of people and a hundred different ways of talking and a hundred different ways of going to church. But they're all American ways.

Understandably many troops, and their parents, regarded Sinatra's patriotism, crafted and burnished thousands of miles from enemy gunfire, as a choice irony. The official explanation given for his absenteeism from the war is that he suffered a perforated eardrum and infection at birth, resulting in chronic mastoiditis that rendered him unfit for military service. At the time, this was widely treated with scepticism. In 1944, Walter Winchell, the popular syndicated newspaper columnist, received an anonymous letter alleging that Sinatra had paid $40,000 to bribe doctors to classify him as medically unfit for service. However, an FBI investigation confirmed that the medical ruling was sound and that no influence was used to prevent him from going to war. Nonetheless, the suspicion that Sinatra's life was too easy and that his gilded status had been attained by devious means took root and diminished his public standing.

Third, rumours began to circulate that Sinatra was embroiled with the Mafia and was a communist infiltrator to boot. To some extent, the origin of these rumours was overtly racist. Sinatra was a first generation Italian-American born into an immigrant neighborhood in Hoboken, New Jersey. For much of middle America this constituted an inherently questionable background, smacking of fancy manners, Mediterranean practices, and shady links with organized crime. During Sinatra's elevation as a celebrity in the late 1930s the controversial execution of two Italian-born anarchists, Nicola Sacco and Bartolomeo Vanzetti, in 1927 was still relatively fresh in people's minds. Sacco and Vanzetti were executed for murdering a clerk and guard in a shoe factory in Braintree, Massachusetts. The evidence against them was circumstantial and during the trial the prosecution focused on their political beliefs, immigrant status, and the fact that they had refused to register for military service under the terms of the Selective Service Act (1917). The episode fueled middle American prejudices that Italian immigrants were freeloaders, work-shy, untrustworthy, and a latent threat to national security. Sinatra himself complained that the charges against him amounted to harassment because his surname ended in a vowel.

But his bravado did not succeed in quelling allegations of links with the Mafia. Indeed, FBI investigations established that Sinatra associated with members of the Mafia in Hoboken, notably Willie Moretti, the *padrino* of New Jersey, and Joe and Rocco Fischetti, known to the FBI as members of Al Capone's Chicago gang. In his defense, Sinatra responded that members of the Mafia were a fixture of several nightclubs in the New Jersey/New York area. As such, it was impossible for entertainers to avoid socializing with them. He emphatically denied that he fraternized with them and dismissed the notion that they played a part in his success as idle conjecture. This did not terminate the rumors.

On some occasions his behavior significantly contributed to them. Most notoriously, Joe Fischetti invited Sinatra to Havana in 1947, ostensibly to entertain the legendary Mafioso Lucky Luciano. Apparently Sinatra failed to realize until too late that he was being lured as cover for the first major gathering of the American Mafia since 1932. Those attending included Frank Costello, Vito Genovese, Augie Pisano, Mike Miranda, Joe Adonis, Joe Profaci, Willie Moretti, Giuseppe "Joe the Fat Man" Magliocco, Albert "the Executioner" Anastasia, Santos Trafficante, Carlos Marcello, Tony Accardo, and Meyer Lansky. The purpose of the meeting was to declare Luciano the head of the American crime syndicate, *capo di tutti capi*. The press fastened upon Sinatra's presence as evidence that he was complicit with the highest echelons of the Mafia machine. Following Luciano's arrest by Cuban officials a week after the meeting, frenzied media coverage was devoted to speculating on the *real* reason behind Sinatra's visit. The proposition emerged that he was carrying $2 million in a suitcase as a tribute to Luciano. Sinatra always denied the charge and protested his innocence. However, the Havana affair sowed the first seeds of suspicion in the public mind that Sinatra's success was at some level fatally implicated with Mafia power.

Condensed with this was a converse set of allegations that painted Sinatra as a communist sympathizer. The late 1940s was the start of deep popular disquiet about the threat posed by the expansionist Soviet empire. Public anxieties about communist infiltration centered on government agencies that ran the country. But the entertainment industry was also scrutinized because it was recognized to be populated by influential figures who possessed the power to shape public opinion. Popular anxieties climaxed with the investigations of Senator McCarthy between 1952 and 1954. However, as early as the mid-1940s, Soviet incursions into Eastern Europe fueled public worries about the "Red Menace." In 1949 Californian Senator Jack B. Tenney released a list of Hollywood celebrities with "Communist leanings." Sinatra was named, together with John Garfield, Katherine Hepburn, Danny Kaye, Gregory Peck, and the *immigré* novelist and winner of the Nobel Prize, Thomas Mann. Senator Tenney's allegations against Sinatra were unparticularized. They reflected a public perception of him as an "immigrant" and a "liberal." He was known to have "advanced" views on full employment and the extension of public schooling through racial integration, and to identify with the civil rights movement. In 1946 he issued a public statement condemning the involvement of the Spanish dictator, Franco, with Hitler and Mussolini. In the same year he served as vice president of the Hollywood Independent Citizens Committee of the Arts, Sciences and Professions (HIC-CASP). This was a broad coalition of pro-Roosevelt liberals and leftists, including Thomas Mann and Rita Hayworth.

These activities hardly amounted to a cast iron case proving Communist leanings.

However, his alleged support for opposition to Congressional contempt citations of the so-called "Hollywood Ten" was potentially more damning. These were screenwriters who, during hearings of the House Un-American Activities Committee (HUAC) in 1947, refused, on First Amendment grounds, to answer questions about their political sympathies and associations. Still, even here support for the Hollywood Ten could be justified as an example of the traditional values of American liberalism inasmuch as it defended the principle of free political conscience. But many were quick to label it a symptom of incipient Trotskyism. In many conservative and middle American circles, Sinatra was guilty by association.

Sinatra's position in American popular culture at this time was far from unassailable. In these years, political and press mutterings about his left-wing views could have fatally damaged his career. However, not for the first or last time, he allowed conviction and hubris to dictate over calm mediation and reflection. He continued his highly public political involvement, as a sponsor, contributor and speaker, with many campaigning organizations, notably the Joint Anti-Fascist Committee, the Free Italy Society, the American Crusade to End Lynching, and the American Society for Cultural Relations with Italy (Meyer 2002: 316). Sinatra's desire to be recognized by the WASP establishment was always counterbalanced by a parvenu's disgust of the trappings of establishment power. It was a recurring tension in Sinatra's public life, and as we shall see, it led to many problems and setbacks in his career.

In a piece written in 1947, Lee Mortimer, a columnist for the Hearst newspaper chain, and nephew of the editor of the Hearst-owned *Mirror* in New York, an acknowledged foe of Sinatra, described *The House I Live In* as "class struggle or foreign *isms* posing as entertainment" (Weiner 1986: 21–2). Circumstantially, Mortimer's argument was reinforced when Albert Maltz, the screenwriter who wrote the script for *The House I Live In*, declined to answer HUAC questions about his association with Communism, and was blacklisted and jailed.

Sinatra's alleged Communist sympathies were also discussed in the columns of the influential show business gossip commentators, Hedda Hopper, Louella Parsons, and Dorothy Kilgallen.

If Sinatra never declared sympathies with Communism, he was open about his support for the New Deal/one nation rhetoric of Franklin D. Roosevelt. In the 1940s it was comparatively unusual for entertainers to declare their political sympathies. The Hollywood studio system sought to create a wholesome, apolitical image of its stable of stars on the calculation that this would maximize box-office appeal and corporate return on investment. From the first, Sinatra was an outspoken critic of class inequality, racism, and unemployment, and an advocate of New Deal politics. In 1943, when riots erupted in Harlem, he spoke to two local schools urging racial harmony and mutual tolerance. Both themes later figured prominently in *The House I Live In*. In 1943 he also travelled to a high school in Gary, Indiana, where disturbances had occurred after the introduction of racial integration policies. Again he condemned racial oppression and made a strong plea for harmony and tolerance.

The right-wing press responded to Sinatra's support for Roosevelt by pejoratively christening him the "New Deal Crooner" (Freedland 1997: 97). Sinatra reacted to right-wing attacks on his alleged political beliefs by writing a two-column letter published in the *New Republic* (Sinatra 1947) which repudiated any connection with Communism. HUAC never subpoenaed him. Furthermore, he was never blacklisted. However, he was cited 12 times in the HUAC hearings, which was more than enough to fuel the fears of the right-wing press that there was something in the notion that Sinatra was a Red (Weiner 1991: 263). In 1954 the Army denied him security clearance to entertain troops in Korea, citing his "Communist affiliations." A year later his application for a passport prompted a full-scale FBI investigation to determine if sufficient evidence existed to warrant prosecution. The 40-page document that emerged from this concluded that no credible evidence existed to connect Sinatra with the Communist Party. Sinatra's protest of innocence and defiance against officialdom appeared to have carried the day.

Ironically, by 1972 any lingering suspicion that Sinatra was a man of the left was erased by his unambiguous identification with the Republican Party. Sinatra now socialized with Richard Nixon, Spiro T. Agnew, and Ronald and Nancy Reagan. At the height of the Red scare, the stage version of *The House I Live In*, initially written and performed as a left-leaning plea for racial tolerance and civil rights, was summarily dropped from his act. However, in 1973 President Nixon called for its reintroduction at a performance at the White House which brought Sinatra out of retirement. Sinatra duly obliged, but transformed the song from a critique of middle American conservative values into a patriotic show-stopper praising the idealized "mom and pop" verities of the American way. In 1991, at the age of 76, he performed it for American troops during the Gulf War. Sinatra's youthful idealistic collectivism had been supplanted by a heroic conservatism, symbolized above all by the prominence given in his repertoire to the song *My Way*, a hoary, sentimental tribute to heroic individualism.

The fourth reason for Sinatra's career slump between 1947 and 1953 is that his choice of music recordings and film performances during this time was often dismal. *The Kissing Bandit* (1948), *The Miracle of the Bells* (1948), *Take Me Out to the Ball Game* (1949), *Double Dynamite* (1951), and *Meet Danny Wilson* (1951) amounted to a run of embarrassing, risible films only lightly punctuated by the relative success of *On The Town* (1949). His parallel recording career fared little better. By the early 1950s, in an attempt to revive his popularity, Mitch Miller, A&R Director of Columbia Records, persuaded Sinatra to record the novelty song *Mama Will Bark*, in which the Sinatra of *Everything Happens to Me* (1941), *I Fall in Love Too Easily* (1944), *Embraceable You* (1944), and *Night and Day* (1947) was required to bark like a dog with a B list, curvaceous comedienne-singer named Dagmar.[3] It is embarrassing evidence of what had come to pass in Sinatra's career. Why was this desperate measure launched?

The early postwar years witnessed the emergence of a substantial, moneyed but temperamental youth market, which
would become more powerful in the 1950s and 1960s under
the impact of full employment. Music executives began to
openly question Sinatra's staying power with the youth market.
By the late 1940s, younger singers like Frankie Laine and
Johnny Ray were comfortably outselling him. Many executives
wondered if Sinatra had become *passé*.

In fact, Sinatra was squeezed between the generations on either
side. Older fans regarded him as too young for them to switch
allegiance from the hardy perennial Bing Crosby, who was releas-
ing one record a week at this time. In addition, Al Jolson, the
veteran white singer who made a fortune in the 1920s and 1930s
by portraying himself as an African-American minstrel, experienced a triumphant comeback. His film *Jolson Sings Again* was
1949's most popular musical. Sinatra was stranded in no man's
land – too young to be accepted by the middle-aged market and
too old to be convincing as a pop idol for teenagers. In 1946 Sinatra
had 15 hit singles. But this success was followed by a long period
in the doldrums, which Sinatra later referred to as "the Dark
Ages." Between 1947 and 1953 none of Sinatra's record releases
reached the top five in the *Billboard* pop chart. Only four singles
made the top ten in 1947, and the number plummeted to one in
1948. Between 1952 and 1953 nothing he released was a hit.

In 1950 the movie mogul Louis B. Mayer cancelled Sinatra's
film contract with Metro-Goldwyn-Mayer. Two years later Columbia Records officially ended his recording contract. By then
some consolation must have been afforded by the inimitable
Ava Gardner, whom Sinatra married in 1951. However, even
this bounty could not disguise the fact that Sinatra's position in
popular culture was in a tailspin. Rejected by MGM and Columbia Records, he sought a deal with RCA, only for the idea to be
dispelled by the sales-people, who rejected him as a has-been.
The music press portrayed the one-year contract he eventually
secured with Capitol Records in 1953 on terribly unfavorable
terms (he received no advance and was required to meet the cost
of recordings from his own pocket) as Sinatra's Gettysburg.

He was 38 years old.

The Elevation of an American Legend

Between 1953 and 1965 Sinatra left behind all canards and innuendos that he was a mere flash in the pan or wartime hit wonder. In these 12 years he established himself as an enduring legend in twentieth-century American popular culture. Within 18 months of the cancellation of his recording contract with Columbia he reversed his career slump. With Ava's connivance he landed the role of the lower-class, victimized New Jersey soldier, Private Maggio, in *From Here to Eternity*. The role, which Sinatra maintained he was born to play, won him an Oscar and rehabilitated him in Hollywood. However, Sinatra regarded movies disparagingly as a sideline. His acting in *From Here to Eternity* (1953), *The Man with the Golden Arm* (1955), *The Joker Is Wild* (1957), *Pal Joey* (1957) and *The Manchurian Candidate* (1962) won a good measure of critical praise. But in general his attitude to movies was strictly instrumental. He regarded them as a lucrative bagatelle. His true vocation and forte lay in vocal performance.

Teamed with a series of fertile, imaginative arrangers at Capitol, above all Nelson Riddle, but also Billy May and Gordon Jenkins, he released a series of classic albums in the 1950s: *In the Wee Small Hours, Songs for Swingin' Lovers, A Swingin' Affair, Only the Lonely, Where Are You?, No One Cares*. More than any other performer, he captured the hedonism, confidence and vulnerability of American consumer culture released from the anxieties and privations of the war years. In songs like *Come Fly with Me, I've Got You Under My Skin,* and *Makin' Whoopee* he transmitted power, assurance, and insouciance. But in other recordings, for example *Lonely Town, One for My Baby, I'll Never Be the Same Again* and *I'm a Fool to Want You*, he radiated the high postwar metropolitan aura of loneliness, displacement, and neurosis.

The best of his Columbia Record releases with the arranger Alex Stordahl in the 1940s – *I Fall in Love Too Easily* (1944), *Saturday Night (Is the Loneliest Night of the Week)* (1945), *These Foolish Things Remind Me of You* (1945), *Day by Day* (1946), *How*

Deep Is the Ocean (1946), *Guess I'll Hang My Tears Out to Dry* (1946) – had had some claim to defining the era. In these songs Sinatra sang like a yearning, rejected, stranded character out of Edward Hopper's film noir masterpiece painting, *Nighthawks* (1942). Their impact was undoubtedly enhanced by Sinatra's unusual capacity to dramatize emotions, especially loneliness and sadness. Some commentators argue that he merely *performed* emotions, implying a fundamental falsity in his artistry (Witkin 2003: 171–2). Undoubtedly, his talents as an actor added distinction to his vocal performances. But there were unstable elements in Sinatra's personality, especially after his final split with Ava Gardner, which lend credence to the popular belief that his best work was from the heart.

Sinatra's lifelong sense of personal restlessness, pensiveness, and inner turmoil is well documented. In the memoir of her father, Sinatra's daughter Tina referred to his death as an "escape" (T. Sinatra 2000: 286). The paradox of an intense sense of dissatisfaction in the midst of outstanding artistic and commercial success is central to understanding Sinatra's relationship to celebrity. In spite of his artistic and material achievement, he never felt a real sense of belonging with the higher echelons of America, while his success cut him off from his roots. Sinatra was a narcissist who believed that his Italian-American background prohibited him from being fully acknowledged by WASP opinion, while his achievements separated him from the values of home. Much of the frustration and rage he displayed throughout his career derived from this painful sense of rejection at the hands of the establishment, twinned with estrangement from the small-town values of Hoboken.

It is also at the core of his violent love of power. Sinatra sought power over others through his involvement with the Mafia, the CIA, prominent politicians and presidents, notably John F. Kennedy and Ronald Reagan. He is alleged to have attempted to destroy the career of his Italian-American, East Coast singing rival Jimmy Roselli (Evanier 2002), and also to employ organized crime to threaten and intimidate people. His violent outbursts, which included many physical attacks on people, lasted

well into his sixties. In his public forays he was often accompanied by a raucous tribe of male drinking companions who acted,
in effect, as his unofficial bodyguards and gleeclub. The clan-
nishness of this group was Sinatra's buffer between the circles of
the Brahmin American power elite and the unsophisticated
melting pot of Hoboken. The membership of this group went
through many phases and changes after its first incarnation in
the 1940s during Sinatra's days with the Harry James Orchestra
and the Tommy Dorsey Band, when it was known as "the
Varsity." By the 1950s and 1960s the main stalwarts were
Hank Sanicola, Sinatra's manager; Bill Miller, his accompanist,
who was known as Sun-Tan Charlie because of his sallow com-
plexion; "Beans" Pondedell, Sinatra's makeup man; Don
McGuire, a journalist; and Jimmy Van Heusen, a songwriter.

Sinatra was a man of immense paradoxes. He chased par-
amours with seigniorial diligence, only to discard them with
caddish abruptness, and often in circumstances that appeared
to be designed to humiliate. He switched his allegiance from
left-liberal politics to the Iron Age conservatism of Richard
Nixon and Ronald Reagan when he judged that by doing so he
might regain the gambling license that was stripped from him in
the early 1960s by the Nevada Gaming Control Board. He relished his identification with pro-Jewish and black civil rights
organizations, but punched Carl Cohen, the casino manager of
Caesar's Palace, and called him a "kike," and "playfully" but
nonetheless racially abused the long-suffering sole black
member of the Rat Pack, Sammy Davis Jr (Taraborrelli 1997:
571; Levy 1998: 113–14). His sexual life, especially in the Rat
Pack years, came close to debauchery, and his violent temper
was the source of repeated public censure. Yet Murray Kempton
called him "puritanical" (1998: 13), and he was easily embarrassed by public displays of bad behavior in others.

By the 1950s Sinatra was cultivating the public face of irrepressible assurance and masculine *joie de vivre* that defined the
rest of his career until the early 1990s, when his health began to
fail. Nowhere more so than in his triumphalist stage act with the
Rat Pack (Dean Martin, Sammy Davis Jr, Peter Lawford, and
Joey Bishop) at the Sands Casino in Las Vegas, in which Sinatra

owned a 2 percent stake which eventually increased to 9 percent. Conversely, in recordings like *Angel Eyes, Willow Weep for Me* and *Mood Indigo,* he answered to America's sense of frailty and vigilance, which in politics was symbolized by Senator Joe McCarthy's crusade against Communism and by the arms race with the Soviets.

Indeed the 12-year span between 1953 and 1965 boasts an embarrassment of riches that left most of his fellow stars of the day in music and film nonplussed. Equally, the remarkable *auteur* albums released in the Capitol years, notably *In the Wee Small Hours* (1955), *Where Are You?* (1957), and *Only the Lonely* (1958), reconceptualized the long-playing record and set new standards in the creation of mood music. In this work Sinatra displayed an artistry and perfectionism that was without parallel in the period. It became the durable basis for the Sinatra legend, which would offset the relative, but highly public, artistic decline he was to suffer between 1973 and 1995. After the difficulties he encountered between 1947 and 1953 it amounted to one of the most remarkable comebacks in postwar American popular entertainment.

The Dark Ages

The period between 1947 and 1953 ranks along with his Italian-American origins as the key to explaining the odd mixture of insouciance and dedication, generosity and hauteur, probity and fraudulence in Sinatra's personality. Plaudits and honors were the preponderant themes in his 60 years as a performer. But the "Dark Ages" were the period in which he was engulfed by the fickle nature of pubic acclaim in all of its unutterable cruelty. At the peak of Sinatra's early success as a solo performer his presence regularly provoked mass hysteria. Over 30,000 youngsters were estimated to have brought midtown Manhattan to a standstill during the so-called "Columbus Day Riot" in 1944 when Sinatra performed at the Paramount theater. The pandemonium required the mobilization of 200 policemen, 20 policewomen, 421 police reserves, 20 radio cars, 2 emergency trucks, 4 lieutenants, 6 sergeants, 2 captains, 2 assistant police inspectors, 2 inspectors, 70 patrolmen, 50 traffic cops, 12 mounted police, and 200 detectives. Yet only four years later, Sinatra had fallen so low that he was widely regarded as yesterday's man. In 1948, Sammy Davis Jr recalled bumping into Sinatra by chance in the center of Manhattan:

> Frank was slowly walking down Broadway with no hat on and his collar up and not a soul was paying attention to him. This was the man who only a few years ago had tied up traffic all over Times Square...Now the same man was walking down the same street and nobody gave a damn. (Quoted in Shaw 1968: 122)

In the lives of celebrities, elevation is often the prologue to a fall from grace, contrition and a bid to gain public forgiveness. Arguably the most famous example in recent times was the late Princess Diana's television revelations about her relationships with Prince Charles and the rest of the royal family. But the phenomenon is quite general in the field of popular entertainment. For example, Judy Garland's battles with alcoholism and substance abuse were accompanied by heartfelt pleas for public understanding. Elizabeth Taylor, Roseanne Barr and Oprah Winfrey battled with weight problems and cited the glare of the spotlight as psychologically damaging. Boy George and Robert Downey Jr asked for public understanding for their struggles with drug addiction. Michael Jackson denied unsavory press allegations about his sexuality and went on record to plead for public understanding about the tensions of stardom. His 2003 interview with Martin Bashir was partly an attempt to rehabilitate his public image, but it went catastrophically wrong when Bashir's interview portrayed a deeply perplexed performer and raised new serious questions about his sexuality and infantilism. Robbie Williams went public with his alcohol and drug addictions in his autobiography *Somebody Someday* and the film *Nobody Someday*. The British variety entertainer Michael Barrymore agreed to a television interview in which he confessed to alcohol and drugs binges.

The conclusion is clear: entertainers who experience a fall from grace make highly public requests for absolution from their fans and the masses. Of course, they are not always successful in this regard. The plea alters the relationship between the celebrity and the public, especially if it is unsuccessful. For example, O. J. Simpson's attempt to rehabilitate himself after being cleared of murder, and Gary Glitter's entreaty for understanding when he was given a prison sentence on a child pornography conviction, fell on deaf ears.

During his career slump between 1947 and 1953 Sinatra reluctantly gave at least two high profile displays of public contrition. At the behest of his long-suffering publicist George Evans, after his brawl with the reporter Lee Mortimer, Sinatra sought public sympathy for his actions via the influential Hollywood gossip columnist, Louella Parsons. In 1947 Evans also persuaded Sinatra to write an open letter to his fans thanking them for support during the press allegations of his involvement with Communism and the Mafia. The letter was reprinted in many magazines and newspapers. Both concessions were out of character. Humility was not a stable feature of Sinatra's personality. In a famous thoughtful interview published in the February 1963 edition of *Playboy*, he described himself as "an 18-carat manic depressive" who "lived a life of violent emotional contradictions" which resulted in "an overacute capacity for sadness as well as elation." The appeals nettled his pride. His bravura code of masculinity, to say nothing of his narcissism, disposed him to be always more willing to offer, insinuate or demand forgiveness than to court it. Unquestionably, when he cultivated Louella Parsons, and solicited support from his fans, it was through gritted teeth.

After Evans's premature death in 1950, Sinatra maintained a relationship with the William Morris talent agency. But he was always a challenge for public relations personnel. His character was truculent, obsessive, imperious, and vain. He did not suffer fools gladly, but having left school early he was always vulnerable and sensitive about "educated" opinion. As he grew wealthier, he became less interested in professional advice and more disposed to follow his nose.

In truth, by the start of the 1960s his position in the entertainment industry appeared to be well-nigh impregnable. He was diversifying his interests from performance to production, through the creation of Reprise records, his investment in the Rat Pack films, and his shares in Nevada gambling casinos. Sinatra had started as an underestimated singer from unfashionable Hoboken. By his mid-forties he was recognized as a stellar artist in both popular music and cinema, and was adding the kudos of being a major budding entertainment tycoon to his hand. Influential publications of the day, such as *American Weekly, Playboy*, and even *Good Housekeeping*, portrayed him as the most powerful player in Hollywood. His vanity responded to the acclaim by slowly adopting a more statesmanlike attitude to achieved celebrity.

The reasons behind this are complex and will be dealt with in greater detail later in the book. To put it simply for the moment, in the incipient years of John F. Kennedy's campaign for the White House, and until 1961 or 1962, Sinatra reveled in the hedonism, iconoclasm and playboy *mien* of the Rat Pack. But by the late 1960s, the rupture in his relations with Kennedy, the rescinding of his Nevada gambling license, and the negative press regarding his dissolute, louche Rat Pack lifestyle produced a significant U-turn in his behavior.

As with much else in his public life, there was a degree of calculation behind this transformation. His attempt to regain his Nevada gambling license amounted to a two decades long campaign which required Sinatra to adopt new levels of decorum and restraint in his public behavior. His involvement in charity work intensified during this time. For example, in April 1962 he embarked on a two-month global charity and goodwill tour. He performed 30 concerts in Japan, Israel, Italy, the UK, Greece, France, and Monaco. The tour raised over a million dollars. Sinatra took it upon himself to pay for the traveling costs and living expenses of all the musicians and his entourage – a sum that is conservatively estimated to have amounted to $200,000, a huge amount by the standards of the day. He also moved from being a prominent supporter of the Democrats to Republican fundraiser. As we shall see in more detail later, Sinatra never

21

mellowed. His character was too truculent and menacing for this to happen. But in the last 25 years of his career he consciously adopted a more statesmanlike persona in the entertainment industry.

"The Least Cooperative Star"

How might one describe Sinatra's behavior before the U-turn in the early 1960s? Throughout his career slump he possessed an extraordinary faith in his absolute uniqueness as a vocalist and in his popular star quality. The music critic Richard Williams (2000: 91) described Sinatra as "the voice of the twentieth century." Sinatra's conviction that he had a unique talent left him impatient with many social conventions. Although this was a lifelong trait, it was especially prominent in his youth and middle age. For two decades after his extraordinary success as a solo performer in the early 1940s, he appears to have regarded his unprecedented artistic and commercial achievements as a license to behave just as he pleased without regard to social convention or, on occasion, legal restraint. For example, he habitually partied through the night, drank to excess, brawled, was intimidating, and was often late on set for filming. He was regularly either cavalier or rebarbative in his relations with directors, producers, and fellow actors. He made promises to the head of MGM, Louis B. Mayer, to entertain the Republican National Conference of State Governors in Sacramento, only to cancel unilaterally, apparently without offering an explanation or an apology. His unguarded and sarcastic comments about Mayer's mistress, Ginny Simms, seem to have been the catalyst behind the termination of his lucrative MGM contract. He was involved in fistfights with columnists and fans. He maintained publicly damaging contact with known members of the Mafia.

In truth, Sinatra exhibited signs of arrogance and contrariness long before the early 1950s. The Women's Press Club voted him "least cooperative star of the year" as early as 1946.[4] The bonhomie that he dispensed to fans and the media during his years with the Harry James Orchestra and the Tommy Dorsey

Band seems to have been cynically contrived. It disguised an unpleasant character blend of excruciating narcissism and brittle intolerance of the prying eye of the public. This was balanced with a tremendous sense of generosity and respect for fellow musicians (Granata 1999). When pressed, Sinatra justified his bad behavior as a reaction to the pressures of stardom. In the 1940s his popularity was certainly phenomenal, and arguably unprecedented. His obituary in the *New York Times* (May 16, 1998) described him not only as "widely held to be the greatest singer in American pop history," but also as "the first modern pop superstar."

Rudy Vallee, Al Jolson and Bing Crosby may actually be considered to have prior claims for this status. Even so, the scale of Sinatra's popularity, especially among the youth audience, was astonishing and certainly brought with it psychological burdens that, in some measure, may account for his ill-judged behavior. With the Tommy Dorsey Orchestra, and after 1942 in the first years of his solo career, Sinatra generated levels of mass hysteria that left major cities paralyzed and the police and press dumbfounded. Aside from the silent film idol Rudolf Valentino (1895–1926), no other popular entertainer before had attracted the same colossal level of female adoration. By degrees humble and insolent, imperious and approachable, sneering and starstruck, Sinatra's behavior provided the template for the later rock aristocracy: Elvis Presley, John Lennon, Bob Dylan, Marvin Gaye, James Brown, Mick Jagger, David Bowie, Robbie Williams, Prince, Tupac Shakur, Liam Gallagher, and Eminem. In the 1940s Sinatra established the role model for the modern pop idol.

During his career slump he displayed the first transparent signs of megalomania that symptomatized much of his later public behavior. Certainly in the conduct of his sexual life he seemed indifferent to either the press or the opinions of middle America. In the early years of Sinatra's elevation as a pop idol, George Evans connived to portray family life with Nancy and the children in the genre of a Norman Rockwell painting, as an idyll of mutual devotion, uxorious fidelity, and family values. In reality, Sinatra was a serial adulterer, conducting innumerable one-night stands and affairs as he toured the US. Most of the time Evans was adroit in concealing Sinatra's infidelity from the public. Yet even he could not prevail upon Sinatra to be more discreet in his relationship with Ava Gardner. When Evans died unexpectedly, Sinatra seems to have decided to forgo all restraint. He persisted with his affair so ardently and with such punitive candor that Nancy filed for separation on Valentine's Day 1950.

Sinatra's relationship with Ava was always volatile. Initially, his recurring worries about her loyalty and respect were relegated behind guilt at the collapse of his marriage. For an unconscionable time after the announcement of the separation from Nancy and the children, his nightclub performances bordered on the unhinged. His violence became unpredictable and was frequently directed against himself. He attempted suicide twice. In 1952 he tried to gas himself in the New York apartment of Manie Sacks, the boss of Columbia Records. Sacks returned just in time to revive him. After his separation from Ava Gardner in 1953 he was found in an elevator at the home of one of his songwriters, Jimmy Van Heusen, with slashed wrists. He also had to have his stomach pumped in 1951 after an allegedly "accidental" overdose of sleeping pills. In these years Sinatra appeared to alternate between wallowing in bottomless despair and pursuing a pathological gangsterish determination to monopolize Ava. He rarely abused his audiences, but he frequently seemed preoccupied, irascible, and distracted. As already noted, even after his marriage to Ava, his recording and film career remained in the doldrums. He attempted to reinvent himself as a television celebrity through the *Frank Sinatra Show* and to return to his roots in radio with *Meet Frank Sinatra*. But the sponsors behind both ventures rapidly canceled after poor audience reaction. Sinatra's career seemed to have something in common with the *Titanic*.

Typically, at this time Sinatra never sought interviews with the media to ask for understanding, insight or forgiveness. If he was plagued by self-doubt and other demons in these years, he withheld his counsel from the press. Unlike the earlier stage in his career, where he was prepared to go through the motions of asking for public forgiveness, he was now above showing contrition. Throughout this period his friends remember him as prone to confusion and emotional turmoil. But, unlike the attempts sponsored by George Evans to gain sympathy earlier in his career, he never explained himself to the public and never seriously sought professional counseling or help.

Italian-American

Sinatra's strong relationship with his mother, Dolly, was certainly a major factor in his extraordinary self-belief. He basked in the light of her unblinking parental devotion. Conversely, he was often exasperated by her domineering, hectoring character. His relationship with Dolly conformed to the stereotypical bond between the only child and its mother in which the adoring mother both inspires and dominates. But Dolly and Frank did not exist in dotlike isolation. As Italian-Americans they occupied a particular habitus, a specific social and cultural ethos which patterned their conduct. Sinatra's preening hauteur, his sentimentality, and his respect for the use of violence conform to a distinctive social-masculine type. This is Sicilian in origin and reveres self-reliance, courage, discretion, and respect from others as role ideals. It is scathing of officialdom, lavishing high praise upon the code of *omerta* – maintaining silence over "crimes" witnessed or experienced. Depending on your point of view, it is either incorrigibly hypocritical or utterly realistic about power, treating public acclaim as both desirable and superficial, and venerating ties of blood and honor as the ultimate bonds that hold society together.

Sicilians display a scornful attitude to aristocracy and inherited status. The self-made man is the idol of the culture, as one might expect in a region that has traditionally wearied under centuries of poverty and oppression at the hands of various colonizing forces. For Sicilians, success is like biblical bread, to be broken and shared rather than monopolized. The man of success is expected to follow the folk principle of *fatti la fame e curcati* - make yourself famous and lie back and relax. But also to be available to the community, and to contribute to the common good. Thus the bravura that is such a dominant part of the masculine code in Sicilian culture has its origins in the recognition of the ultimate greater importance of community.

In middle age, Sinatra certainly cultivated this facade. The Rat Pack was an extended tribute to the values of hedonism, optimism and easy living. But it also proffered protection, assistance and solidarity to those involved with it. In hindsight it can be interpreted as a repudiation of the WASP values of discretion, thrift and self-control upon which the hegemonic ideal of American masculinity was constructed. Against this, the Rat Pack reveled in conspicuous consumption, immediate gratification, whisky-soaked priapism, leisurely rounds of golf, and helping a buddy. Traditionally, the nouveaux riches in America emulated the values and lifestyles of the establishment. Parvenus like Sinatra, Dean Martin and Sammy Davis Jr understood the convention. For example, their dress and grooming was the best that money could buy. Their image as sybarites was balanced by copper-bottomed patriotism. They extolled the American way and brandished the unfortunate national introspection with regard to world affairs. For these men, four of whom were of immigrant stock, America was the best of all possible worlds – arguably a delusion still shared by most Americans.

As is the fashion with the celebritariat in America, they and their wives also generously gave their money and spare time to appropriate charitable causes. But throughout they complained of establishment condescension. To repeat: four of the Rat Pack were the offspring of immigrant parents. Even the fifth member, Sammy Davis Jr, who possessed the best credentials of a truly American pedigree, had a Puerto Rican-born mother, Elvera "Baby" Sanchez. Sammy was also, of course, black. In all of them, the understandable pleasure in achievement was counterbalanced by a stubborn feeling of displacement. Although their wealth brought them to the ramparts of the American establishment, their status as nouveaux riches was always problematic. One reason why Sinatra so relished playing the part of Major

Ben Marco in his favourite movie role, in *The Manchurian Candidate* (1962), is that the brainwashed Marco eventually exposes both his Korean controllers *and* their establishment puppets, John and Eleanor Iselin (played by James Gregory and Angela Lansbury). The moral is that the establishment is always rotten, a prejudice shared by the downtrodden and the parvenu class alike. For Sinatra, ordinary, decent Americans who seek to achieve according to the meritocratic ideal laid down by the founding fathers, are sure to encounter the canker of deceit and self-interest which lies at the heart of the power hierarchy. Arguably, this is one reason for his notably relaxed attitude to the Mafia, who sought to realize the American dream by illegal activity.

At this juncture one must pause to reflect that at least part of Sinatra's insufferable self-righteousness and shallow didacticism, as well as his impulse towards generosity and antiracism and his abhorrence of flummery and humbug, was the result of his naive innocence in believing in America as an ideal. This was also the motive behind his lifelong patriotism and inconstant party politics. It is easy to discount the point. But for immigrants of Sinatra's day, and arguably even in contemporary times, America represented a clean slate, an arena for personal advancement and the realization of discredited eighteenth-century European ideals of liberty, fraternity and equality. Adherence to roots might be a dogmatic matter to their parents, but for the "first born" Americans of Sinatra's generation nothing was written in stone, everything was possible. For all his sense of being, at a fundamental level, misplaced in America, of not quite understanding the rules of the game, Sinatra savored these values, regarding them as defining the American way in distinction from exhausted and tarnished European precedents.

The children of first born white immigrants exist in a peculiar liminal space that has perhaps not received sufficient attention in academic literature. For these people – in Sinatra's day, as perhaps still today – are peculiarly displaced figures. The language of the idealized "society" differs from the language of home, not merely in respect of class and ethnic codes and conventions, but more fundamentally in respect of vocabulary, syntax, shared understanding, and practices of embodiment. Although participation in schooling, work, sport, and wider popular culture acculturates them to the mores and values of the host society, they regard themselves as a violently trans-planted species, bedded into strange soil, carrying folk beliefs, ways of speaking, ways of seeing and ways of embodiment that are not universally understood. They can never be truly "Ameri-can" because their physical features, habits of comportment and "native" understanding irretrievably betray older, abandoned origins. Even successful Caucasian immigrants catch themselves feeling that they inhabit a different skin, one that is ritually denigrated by WASP America.

Sinatra wrestled with this for most of his life. His assiduous courting of politicians, his determination to entertain troops overseas after World War Two despite his initial, deep unpopu-larity with servicemen, his rheumy patriotism, his involvement with prominent politicians, can all be interpreted as attempts to acquire legitimacy. But his judgment in these matters was often faulty. Finally, he was too worldly to accept the premise that America is utopia. But paradoxically he held fast to the myth that America is, after all the wheeling and dealing, the crossing and the double-crossing, the best of all possible worlds. It is a common fancy, not only of migrant Americans but also of long-rooted stock. In a sense, the Minotaur of Sina-tra's adult life was the chasm between the purple promise of new life in America and the daily example and experience of the disappointed upwardly mobile, the frustrated, and the cruelly deceived.

The "Jack Pack" and its Consequences

The most notorious and, for Sinatra, suppurating example of this was his association with the Kennedys, especially during the presidential campaign of 1960. By common consent, Sinatra played a highly active, effective role in John F. Kennedy's elec-tion campaign. He marshaled the Rat Pack to offer public support for Kennedy at the Democratic national convention in Los Angeles and participated in fundraising and publicity endorsement. At this time the Rat Pack was momentarily rechristened the "Jack Pack." They sang the *Star-Spangled Banner* and refrained from rising to racist taunts from Mississippi bigot delegates who protested at Sammy Davis Jr's presence on stage. The Sinatra song *High Hopes*, with new lyrics by Sammy Cahn, was adopted as Kennedy's campaign tune. After victory, Sinatra organized the presidential gala to celebrate Kennedy's election.

Yet within a year he was branded as a high-risk associate by Robert Kennedy and banished from the White House. Nick Tosches, the estimable biographer of Dean Martin, pointedly contrasts Martin's careful distance from the Kennedys with Sinatra's primitive first born American devotion. "Dean," writes Tosches cuttingly, "saw what Sinatra was too blind to see: there was no place in Camelot for wops" (1992: 331).

This is too brutal. The Kennedy's were sensitive to racism and bigotry, not least because the presidential campaign had been mired with anti-Irish and anti-Catholic jibes. Outwardly their politics was post–New Deal ecumenical, offering all peoples, of all creeds and colors, an equal share in democracy. But, of course, above all they were keenly interested in votes. Their support for the civil rights movement was at least in part calculated to deliver the black vote in the 1964 election. By extension, after 1961 they spurned Sinatra because his reputation for consorting with the Mafia made him an electoral liability. For Sinatra, the episode merely confirmed his conviction that despite his wealth and artistic achievements, as an Italian-American he would always be persona non grata in the eyes of the American establishment. The decision of the Nevada Gaming Control Board to rescind his gambling license and close his Cal-Neva casino in 1963 poured salt into the wound. After the mid-1960s it was the spur behind his philanthropic work and, arguably, the key factor in his drift to the right in the 1970s. Sinatra was possessed of a fierce sense of injustice, a burning insistence that he was above the judgment of ordinary people or elected officials, and a stinging conviction that he would never be fully accepted by the elite in American society.

American Caesar

After 1953, Sinatra became an American Caesar: king of the Rat Pack, champion of the public, and dictator to the press. His songs entered the vernacular of both elite and popular culture, in the way that poetry used to before the invention of the phonograph. Indeed the songs that Sammy Cahn and Jimmy Van Heusen wrote for him *were* the poetry of American consumer culture in the 1950s. This was astounding success. The mass mania that Elvis Presley generated with teenagers in the 1950s, and that the Beatles and Rolling Stones surpassed in the 1960s, was not what he was seeking, although despite this he seldom ducked a chance to be scathing about it. He had been in the same position in the early 1940s and was a pastmaster at appreciating the fickle, transient nature of achieved celebrity, especially in the youth culture market. Real staying power lay in dominating the charts for decades not years. Despite flirting with pop and rock music later in his career by recording *Strangers in the Night, Love Me Tender, Yesterday, Something,* and *Mrs Robinson*, Sinatra held the bass, rhythm guitar, lead guitar and drums combination in low esteem. When he founded Reprise records in 1961 he declined to sign rock acts. Rock'n'roll signified not only the rude ascendance of the new, inscrutable youth culture market, it also smacked of levels of spontaneity and indiscipline that, in Sinatra's day, had perhaps not been seen since the Roaring Twenties.

It especially irked him that he was no longer perceived as holding the finger on the pulse of the youth market. For Sinatra, being viewed as cool and hip was fundamental and nonnegotiable. In his mind the rise of rock'n'roll symbolized the final end of the big band/nightclub era with all of its elegance and coruscating repartee, in which he had proven himself to be a seminal exemplar. Accordingly, his view of rock performers was acerbic and uncharitable. For example, in an interview given in 1957 he excoriated the music of the Elvis Presley generation of performers thus:

It is sung, played and written for the most part by cretinous goons and by means of its almost imbecilic reiterations and sly, lewd – in fact plain dirty – lyrics ... it manages to be the martial music of every sideburned delinquent on the face of the earth. (Quoted in Evanier 2002: 89)

This was at best ingenuous and at worst hypocritical. As he set out on a solo career in 1942, Sinatra was an overtly sexual performer, caressing the microphone and standing in a suggestive manner, and using his peerless powers of enunciation to seduce the largely female audiences. For Sinatra, real vocal art lay in a singer fronting a big band and holding an audience in the palm of his hand by intonation, timing, and above all, enunciation. It was in the late 1950s and early 1960s that he engraved himself indelibly upon the public mind as the greatest living exponent of his art.

In part this was achieved by his sheer cultural *persistence* in the 1950s and 1960s. By today's standards, his work-rate and level of output was extraordinary:

- 3 releases of long-players per year in 1958, 1959
- 4 releases of long-players per year in 1960, 1961, 1963, 1965
- 6 releases of long-players per year in 1964
- 7 releases of long-players in 1957, 1962

All of this was accomplished in tandem with a film career that was equally demanding:

- 5 full-length feature films in 1955
- 4 full-length feature films in 1956
- 3 full-length feature films per year in 1957, 1960, 1962, 1965, 1966
- 2 full-length feature films per year in 1958, 1959, 1964, 1967

For a figure notorious in popular culture as much for his sybaritism and hedonism as his artistry, this was a record of remarkably industrious output.

Of course, not all of it was of the highest order. Despite their commercial success, *Come Fly with Me* (1958) and *Come Dance with Me* (1959) are, in my view, below-par albums. *Come Fly with Me* is a lightweight concoction, cashing in on the boom in long-distance air travel. The mediocrity is only relieved by an outstanding version of *April in Paris*. *Come Dance with Me* is disengaged and liberally douched with counterfeit nostalgia. Both recordings were long hits with the public. *Come Fly with Me* held the number one spot for five weeks and was in the top 50 for 70 weeks; *Come Dance with Me* won a Grammy award for best album recording of the year. However, like most of his recordings after 1973, both albums smack of Sinatra trying to second-guess contemporary taste but ending up patronizing his audience or unintentionally reminding them of former glories.

As for his film output, Sinatra was highly inconsistent. He followed up the artistic and commercial successes of *The Man with the Golden Arm* (1955), *The Joker Is Wild* (1957), and *The Manchurian Candidate* (1962) with lowbrow pabulum of the order of *Johnny Concho* (1955), *Never So Few* (1959), and *Come Blow Your Horn* (1963).

Although in these years Sinatra repeatedly returned to the high theme of using popular art to change culture, his choice of projects was mercurial. He rarely passed up the chance of making a quick buck. This appears to have been the dominant motive in Sinatra's involvement in instantly forgettable films like *The Pride and the Passion* (1957), *Can-Can* (1960), *Sergeants Three* (1961), *Robin and the Seven Hoods* (1964), *Marriage on the Rocks* (1965), *Assault on a Queen* (1966), and *Dirty Dingus Magee* (1970); and formulaic albums like *Cycles* (1968), *A Man Alone* (1969), and *Some Nice Things I've Missed* (1974).

The Generalissimo of Romance

Interestingly, if Sinatra was a somewhat cavalier "natural" actor, seldom bothering to suffer more than two takes of a scene, he was never less than a dedicated vocalist. Commentators maintain that he was more adept than other vocalists at persuading individual members of the audience that he was singing directly to them. They refer to Sinatra's warmth and common touch. What is not often pointed out is that Sinatra never approached the audience as an equal. Even in the final decade of his performing career, when his broken health obliged him from time to time to approach his audience as a hoary old generalissimo rather than the concupiscent Lothario of yore, he retained an imposing demeanor. The demotic, participatory styles developed by younger singers in the 1960s and 1970s were anathema to him. Sinatra always remained aloof, a fact that his fans neutralized in their eagerness to acknowledge him as "one of us." His intonation, timing and use of counterpoint conveyed power, magnanimity and a carefree existence, but the content of his songs often spoke of rejection, frustration and solitude.

This also applied to his onstage repartee. He projected a bravura masculine lifestyle of guiltless promiscuity and conspicuous consumption, yet his life seemed so fundamentally unfulfilled that at the end of it, his daughter Tina remarked: "He was ready to go. He was so tired and lonely and broken. His soul had expired years before that stubborn body gave way. His future held nothing but pain. He could never be at peace, never stop running, until he *stopped*" (T. Sinatra 2000: 286, emphasis in original).

Sinatra reflected the central values of American postwar consumer culture. That is, an unwavering faith in the American way, a belief that economic growth will eventually solve the fundamental social problems in society, an expectation that scientific, medical and technological advance will eventually make life easier for everyone, and a conviction that American democracy was the best political system devised by man. He also understood the corruption of American economic and political life, and the truth in the cliché that Hollywood is a boulevard of broken dreams. Sinatra regarded himself to be the unelected representative of ordinary people and he often commented on social and political issues. Despite the shift to the right in the last three decades of his life, his political philosophy remained true to the Panglossian model outlined in the short didactic film he made in 1945, *The House I Live In*. It consisted of the patriotic belief that America is genuinely the land in which people of different creeds and colors can live together in mutual peace, tolerance and harmony, and where opportunity abounds.

But it is articulated from a position of great wealth, cultural privilege, and firsthand knowledge of political chicanery and economic manipulation. Sinatra's celebrity conferred upon his actions a certain level of immunity. He expatiated oleaginously on American inclusiveness and justice, while conducting a life that involved business deals with known members of the Mafia, sexual libertinism, and frequent acts of physical violence.

Garry Wills has remarked of the right-wing movie star John Wayne that he was an "American Adam" (1997: 302). By this he meant that Wayne's patriotism, masculinity and image of rugged self-reliance transcended postrevolutionary East Coast American dreams of drawing-room sophistication by renewing the ideal of the vigorous frontiersman, the "true" American, ever vigilant and ever situated on the boundary of the expanding West, looking outward. At the heart of this is a biblical sense of the original man, stripped of connotations of class, status and race, who makes his own way, by his own codes, which nonetheless reflect the utopian mores of America.

In contrast, Sinatra is a much more worldly example of achieved American celebrity. He enters the public eye in the late 1930s as a callow youth who is somehow well versed in the politics of seduction, manipulation and violence. Even his early image of vulnerable, unspoilt youth contained the seeds of corruption and venality. The first public signs of this were perhaps the intimidating manner he adopted with the press. According to the *Washington News* (April 14, 1947), as early as 1946 he threatened, albeit by telegram, to give the Hollywood columnist Erskine Johnson "a belt in your vicious and stupid mouth." The *New York Times* (April 14, 1947), reporting the assault on the columnist Lee Mortimer at Ciro's restaurant, quoted Sinatra as saying: "For two years he's been needling me. He gave me a look. I can't describe it. It was one of those contemptuous 'Who do you amount to' looks. I followed him outside. I hit him." This assault occurred in the same year as Sinatra's damaging summit with leading figures of the Mafia in Havana. It prefigured the intimidation, belligerence and arrogance that blighted his public reputation in his middle and later years.

Caesarism is a condition of authority marked by supreme self-confidence, reticence about motives, steadfastness, self-absorption, and elevation above all customary ties and connections. It mixes generosity of spirit with frosty determination and an audacious indifference to public opinion (Meier 1996). Society does not have much hold upon Caesar, since his accomplishments have elevated him high above the conventions and mores of ordinary life. Conversely, elevation induces a state of languor in the achieved celebrity. Narcissism is emotionally isolating because the tributes of the people never quite match what the narcissist believes is his due. To fill the gap the narcissist seeks new sensations, but their failure to satisfy reinforces the tendency toward introversion and melancholy. The outside world is the source of the narcissist's *substance*, but it is a world that he regards as ever more unworthy and fetid. Hence the recourse to reckless behavior as a way of proving independence and superiority. Hence also the contrary tendency toward altruism and generosity. All of this applied to Sinatra in his middle and old age.

He regularly helped friends in need with all-expenses-paid holidays. After Charlie Morrison, owner of the Mocambo nightclub in Hollywood, died suddenly, Sinatra took it upon himself to pay his debts and provide for his dependants. When Bela Lugosi was hospitalized for his drug addiction, Sinatra paid his bills. When the actor Lee J. Cobb suffered a major heart attack, Sinatra, who had little more than a nodding acquaintance with him, put Cobb in a rest home for six weeks at his own expense. Later he installed him as his house guest in Palm Springs, found him an apartment in Los Angeles, and paid all of his bills until he resumed his career. When Buddy Rich, the drummer with whom Sinatra had a major fight in the Tommy Dorsey days, suffered a serious heart attack, Sinatra assumed responsibility for all of his medical expenses (Levinson 1999: 209).

Sinatra's generosity in his charity work could be even more extravagant. In 1970, Sinatra and Count Basie gave two concerts at the Royal Festival Hall in London. The entire proceeds of both performances were donated to children's charities. Moreover, Sinatra paid for the accommodation and expenses of not only his own entourage but all of the Basie band (Shaw 1968: 7).

Without wishing to minimize the authenticity of Sinatra's generosity, the gift can be read as the narcissist's way of showing his elevation from worldly things. It provides another basis for tributes, but it also underline's the narcissist's ultimate indifference to materialism. The narcissist finds no one to attach himself to since, by definition, he is without equal. The psychological remedy to this overpowering sense of a gap from others and the inner emptiness of being singular is twofold. On the one hand, the narcissist devotes himself or herself to sealing their own perfection through accomplishments that are consciously designed to be epochal and thus a perpetual reminder to others of superiority. On the other hand, the narcissist surrenders himself or herself to passionate distractions as a way to forget the uneasiness and discontent of their inner life. Ava Gardner's "otherness" is an example of this. Her attraction for Sinatra was proportionate to her power to destroy him, a power he romantically chose to see as beyond reason. This accurately describes the real public and private face of Frank Sinatra. By the mid-1950s he had become an American Caesar, and the melancholy, despairing side of his character was as solidly formed as his regal public bearing.

Sinatra and the Technology of Popular Entertainment

Vocal performance was Sinatra's forte and he was obsessive in his technical perfectionism. In fact, he was always more a technician than a natural singer. He worked on breath control, elocution and enunciation. In his youth he swam every day to increase his lung capacity, and he was not simply a fan of Bing Crosby, Billie Holiday and Mabel Mercer, he *studied* them to learn how they achieved their musical effects.

Some of his most important influences are unexpected. From Jascha Heifetz, he noticed that the violin player moved his bow over the fiddle and back again without seeming to pause, and he applied the technique to singing. He copied the mouth control and breathing technique of the trombone player and band leader Tommy Dorsey, to allow him to take a breath while singing. Sinatra developed a consummate style of legato singing that enabled him to dramatize melodies and words so as to achieve maximum impact. His repeated displays of arrogance, grandeur and insufferable rudeness, which, it must be said in mitigation, alternated with extraordinary acts of generosity and genuine magnanimity, derived most forcefully from his conviction that he was unsurpassed in his calling. By the late 1960s, his addictions to Jack Daniels, nicotine and high living would take their toll on his voice. But the confidence and zest that he achieved in both his recordings and film performances during his peak years provided American popular culture with a powerful post-war model of invincible authority in the genre of mass popular entertainment.

Sinatra belonged to the first generation of performers and consumers who regarded the electronic media as a staple form of popular entertainment. In eighteenth-century Europe the distinction between high and low forms of entertainment was not strong. The notion that musical literacy is a prerequisite of musical appreciation cohered in the early nineteenth century. Of course, the aristocracy always possessed free time. But it was permeated with the, often sullen, recognition of tacit seigniorial responsibilities and duties that generally hindered their freedom. While there was some basis in fact for the stereotypes of the dissolute duke and the ethically challenged earl, there was also a basic inertia in feudal society where many traditional rights and obligations remained immovably hallowed by time. With the ascendancy of the rising industrial and business class, appreciation of the arts of vocal and instrumental performance was venerated as a mark of high social status. It differentiated the capital-owning class from propertyless laborers and it established divisions of taste and *Kultur* within the ranks of the ascendant class. The schism between highbrow and lowbrow cultural forms became pronounced. The children of the nouveaux riches cultivated knowledge of the musical arts as part of their spectrum of self-improving pastimes. The romantic ideal of the artist as a tortured, passionate performer was embodied in the careers of Niccolò Paganini (1782–1840) and Franz Liszt (1811–1886). The creation by Richard Wagner (1813–1883) of the Bayreuth theatre as a temple of superior musical art symbolized the triumph of the "refined" art of the industrial and aristocratic classes. These models of achieved celebrity were implacably hierarchical, since they positioned "genius" as the mark of God that separates the artist from the people (Hughes 1974; Frith 1998).

Sinatra did not spring from these social strata. His parents were Italian immigrants. Both were keenly aware of status distinctions from old Europe relating to cultural capital and position. Dolly Sinatra's parents immigrated from Genoa, and they regarded the Sicilian stock from which Sinatra's father, Marty, hailed as an inferior class. Sinatra was not raised in a hothouse of artistic aspiration. His parents were upwardly mobile, but the arts and musical performance did not figure prominently in family pastimes. However, an understanding of the relationship between taste and authority was well anointed in his family background. Sinatra's obsessive concern with appearance and cleanliness – throughout his life he changed his clothes and showered several times a day – and his preoccupation with social position and rank fully reflect his original social milieu. It is also evident in the honor that he attributed to singing. Sinatra's sense of vocation was hewn from the same ideology of artistic achievement as that observed in high culture. As a performer he sought to be without equal. In his finest recordings he aimed not merely to entertain, but to leave a permanent cultural mark as an artist. The public face of his celebrity showed few signs of this in the early years of his career. By the mid-1950s it was an overt feature of his stage act and recording career. It forms the backdrop to his middle career and later years and is the standard by which his work should be judged.

Sinatra's first contact with commercial live musical performance was vaudeville. Vaudeville developed in America as a form of popular variety entertainment in the late 1880s. From its ranks emerged popular stars like Al Jolson, Mae West, the Marx Brothers, W. C. Fields, and Bob Hope. Sinatra's stage act with the Rat Pack in the 1950s borrowed some of the classic motifs and routines of high vaudeville. However, by the time he reached his mid teens vaudeville was in precipitous decline. New forms of popular entertainment at a remove from live performance, notably radio, film and gramophone recording, were taking over.

Radio was an especially important influence. The formation of NBC in 1927 and CBS in 1928 offered audiences round-the-clock variety, coast to coast. Sinatra gained his first indelible insights into the ideology of artistic success from radio and film. His idols were not Wagner and Brahms, although interestingly Sinatra enjoyed classical music, especially the work of Vaughan Williams, but the pop gods of his day: Bing Crosby, Rudy Vallee, and Fred Astaire. They supplied him with his earliest images of the glamour of achieved celebrity and the power of artistic success. Big bands and swing music became popular phenomena in the 1930s. Between 1933 and 1938 sales of RCA Victor recordings increased by 600 per cent.

Radio introduced Sinatra to the Benny Goodman Band and the Tommy Dorsey Orchestra, with whom he would eventually feature as lead singer. It offered the adolescent Sinatra a staple and cheap means of musical education and of learning how to read mass taste. It was also the direct instrument for his initial success. In his teens Sinatra participated in amateur talent contests run in local vaudeville theaters like the Central in Jersey City and the Fabian in Hoboken. Sinatra's victory in a "Future Stars" contest in the latter venue led to an appearance at a downtown Manhattan vaudeville house, the Academy of Music on 14th Street. Through this route Sinatra made the acquaintance of other young hopefuls in the music business. He eventually founded a singing group, called the Hoboken Four. Their victory in September 1935, on a leading NBC talent show called *Major Bowes and His Original Amateur Hour* broadcast from the Capitol Theater, New York, was decisive in launching him on the road to stardom.

The programme was a classic example of how radio juxtaposed and blended different musical genres and eroded the barrier between highbrow and lowbrow forms of entertainment. For example, the *Major Bowes* show also launched the careers of future stars of New York's Metropolitan Opera like Beverly Sills and Robert Merrill. Discretion was not a prominent part of Sinatra's personality and he could be scathing in public about Bowes himself. During a monologue on the *Sinatra at the Sands* album, recorded with the Count Basie Orchestra in 1966, he described Bowes as "a pompous bum with a bulbous nose. He used to drink Green River. He was a big drunk, was Bowes. I don't know if you've heard of Green River, but it takes the paint off your deck if you got a boat! 59 cents a gallon baby!"

However, the *Major Bowes* show was not the *Pop Idol* of its day. Victory did not result in a cash prize or a lucrative recording contract. Instead, the Hoboken Four joined the *Major Bowes* traveling show, earning $50 a week plus meals. The unit toured as far away as Hollywood, and there was constant artistic and personal friction between Sinatra and the other members of the group. They disbanded acrimoniously, and Sinatra returned to the grind of amateur talent contests and small club bookings in New Jersey.

Without radio Sinatra would still have been a major icon in twentieth-century popular culture. But its popular growth coincided with Sinatra's teens and enabled him to develop distinctive new ways of marketing himself as a pop idol. Sinatra was 14 when the popular singer Rudy Vallee became a radio sensation through his appearances on radio's first hour-long variety show, *The Fleischman Hour*. He was also aware of the impact that his idol Bing Crosby had achieved through the medium. Accordingly, as he relaunched his career as a solo performer in 1936, he offered to sing for free in local radio stations in New Jersey and New York. Sinatra made informal surveys of the listening habits of radio audiences. He divided them into four groups: the early morning birds, the lunchtime devotees, the teatime gang, and the insomniacs. He tailored his pitch to radio executives to gain airway time accordingly.

His obsession with gaining airtime by any means led to him singing at the Rustic Cabin Roadhouse on Route 9W near Alpine, New Jersey. The venue possessed a radio wire. This was a long-term engagement in which Sinatra sang solo, performed with an ensemble group called the Three Flashes or Pages, emceed, and sometimes waited on tables for $15 a week. Sinatra's months at the Rustic Cabin coincided with the proliferation of big bands in the New York area. The Paul Whiteman Dance Band held popular residencies at the Biltmore Hotel, the Jimmy Dorsey Band had a similar slot at the Pennsylvania Hotel, Guy Lombardo was at the Roosevelt, and Glen Miller's band was playing at the Glen Island Casino. Harry James, who formed his band in 1939 as an offshoot from the Benny Goodman Orchestra, discovered Sinatra at the Rustic Cabin in March 1939. He signed him on a $75 a week contract as lead vocalist. In addition to touring the East Coast, the Mid West and the West Coast, Sinatra participated in five recording sessions with the Harry James Orchestra, one of which yielded the crucial hit, *All or Nothing at All*. This recording is alleged to have caught the interest of Tommy Dorsey, who poached Sinatra to be the lead vocalist of his own, more popular band in December of 1939.

Sinatra's early success with the Tommy Dorsey Band was predicated in the image of a skinny kid emerging from the anonymous ranks of the listening public. He portrayed himself as an ordinary Joe, blessed with a mellifluous singing voice but essentially no different from the other decent kids in prewar and wartime American consumer culture. This was an act of calculated affectation. Sinatra always held a high, not to say Olympian, regard for his gifts. Throughout his career he played with the motif of being an ordinary Joe, but in reality he was an unusually imperious achieved celebrity, holding most other performers and often the listening public in low esteem.

Sinatra's belligerence and fastidiousness were already well established in his days with Dorsey. At a concert in Omaha he physically threatened a member of the audience who threw popcorn on to the stage during the performance. One evening, backstage at the Astor Roof, he had an altercation with the drummer Buddy Rich, hurling a pitcher of water at the player with such ferocity that pieces of the glass were embedded in the plaster. At the same time, he insisted on staying at the best hotels during tours, often breaking with the band to do so. Band members recall him as always being impeccably dressed. He insisted on having two or three showers a day, and generally requested his pay to be handed over in new bills. His traveling cases were meticulously organized, with each item in place and precisely folded (Shaw 1968: 33–4).

Sinatra enjoyed increased radio exposure with the Tommy Dorsey Band and this was crucial in constructing the emerging public face of Sinatra as a mass celebrity. But he was also fortunate in achieving public acclaim as a singer when the technology of vocal performance was undergoing massive transformation. Edison patented the microphone in 1886. However, its development as an indispensable accessory in vocal performance took many years. Sinatra himself began singing with a megaphone. The microphone revolutionized stage performance. At a stroke it removed the requirement for singers to sing in high ranges in order to be heard above the band. Crucially, it enabled amplification to be rendered compatible in performance with the representation of intimacy. Whispers and sighs became audible, thus adding to the conversational, personalized tone. Singers no longer appeared to sing *at* the audience but engaged in an exchange *with* them. Most critics credit Bing Crosby with being the first popular vocalist to realize the auditory potential of the microphone on stage. But Sinatra was the first popular performer to use it as an *instrument*. In gripping the stationary mike, stroking it from side to side, Sinatra suggested erotic foreplay. "You must never jar the audience with it," he explained (quoted in Lahr 1998: 17). "You must know when to move away from the mike and when to move into it . . . It's like a geisha girl."

His performance also suggested the vulnerability of callow youth – a crucial asset in an era when many mothers, sisters and girlfriends were all too aware of the sacrifices being made by young American males in the fight against fascism. In the words of Shaw:

[Sinatra] did not gesture, swing his hips, stamp his feet or leap in the air. He just stood at a microphone, clutching it as if he were too frail to remain standing without it. But the mike mannerism, the limp curl, the caved-in cheeks, the lean hungry look – "the frightened smile" as one reporter put it – emphasized a boyish-ness that belied a wife and child and brought him as close as the boy next door. (1968: 47)

The intimacy that Sinatra was able to build with an audience was a priceless asset in his popularity. Later, in the 1950s, with the introduction of 12-inch rather than 10-inch long-players Sinatra would transform the album experience. He used the longer playing times to develop a concept or narrative line. Indeed, Sinatra has some claim to be the inventor of the concept album. When he began his recording career in 1938 standard records were produced in the 78 rpm form of a single. Albums were available, but only in the cumbersome and expensive format of several 78s stored in a cardboard holder. Sinatra's first album, *The Voice*, was released in this version. Unfortunately, because the major record labels were geared up for the singles market, and because *The Voice* carried a high retail price, sales were disappointing.

The plastic microgroove long-playing record was launched in 1948 by Columbia records. The first long-players were in the 10-inch format, and a rerelease of *The Voice* was one of the first Columbia products. From today's standpoint the 10-inch tech-nology was Neanderthal. They allowed for only four or five songs on each side. The 12-inch version which became widely available in the mid-1950s permitted eight songs each side. The first releases of LPs of both types suffered because the market for record players that could play them was in its infancy, but they would eventually transform the record business.

Sinatra's recordings in the 1950s demonstrated an alert, well-informed and imaginative interest in the new technology. *The Voice* is arguably the first concept album inasmuch as the indi-vidual recordings are clearly selected to combine into a single mood for the listener. But his albums of the mid to late 1950s, notably *In the Wee Small Hours* (1955), *Where Are You?* (1957) and *Only the Lonely* (1958), move beyond *mise-en-scène* mood-setting to play a didactic role. In these albums Sinatra seeks to share his personal experience of frustrated love and the thwarted ideals of youth. These albums convey the impression that difficulties in love are universal and that Sinatra is a Zen master of the game. At the same time, Sinatra portrays himself as the very generalissimo of rejection. The young Sinatra of *I Fall in Love Too Easily* (1944), *She's Funny That Way* (1944) and *I Don't Stand a Ghost of a Chance* (1945) was role-playing. He was imagining the possibilities of romantic bliss and catastrophe as all young lovers do. The classic albums of the mid to late 1950s deliberately articulate his own experience and tacitly assume that his listeners have knowledge of his love life through the media. In all of them Ava Gardner is obviously the siren figure, whose appetites and impulses are a source of delight that cannot be controlled or collared and therefore cannot be relied upon. These are albums conceived and performed exclusively from the masculine standpoint. Sinatra is concerned not merely to share the experience of rejection, but to create a frame for it that conclusively defines the experience in popular culture. "Make it one for my baby, and one more for the road" is a grace note for the postwar male experience of bewilderment about the labyrinth of liberated femininity. These albums provide not merely a reflection of popular culture, but a reading of it that qualifies them as durable art.

Achieved Celebrity and the Microscope of the Public

The influence of technology upon Sinatra's art cannot be exaggerated. He was one of the first wave of pop idols to acquire fame in the age of fully developed consumer culture. For achieved celebrities of his generation the sense of living life in the public eye was unprecedented. Artists in high print culture during the late nineteenth century maintained a sense of privacy. They sequestered their private lives from public scrutiny and generally were more successful in defending a distinction between their private (or veridical) self and the public face. This was necessary for maintaining psychological equilibrium. For achieved celebrities of Sinatra's day, the distinction was no longer tenable. Radio, film and later television and video were added to the probing hand of print culture to place them permanently under the public microscope. Achieved celebrities began to complain of being engulfed by their public image. To some extent, their sense of a private self was erased. Their position and wealth was subject to the fickle nature of the public. For this reason, performers often developed a love/hate relationship with their fans.

Naturally, as he aged, Sinatra's position under the microscope of the public changed. There is no question that unadulterated female lust was a major factor in the mass hysteria generated during his time with the Harry James Orchestra (1939), the Tommy Dorsey Band (1939–42), and especially in the first years of his solo career. The young Sinatra availed himself of the sexual opportunities that fame provided. In fact he did so greedily throughout his career until his early sixties, when, according to one of his biographers, his years of heavy drinking and high living rendered him impotent (Taraborrelli 1997: 580–1). Unquestionably, his behavior confirmed Freud's view that male artistic endeavor is driven by the desire for fame, wealth, and the love of beautiful women (Freud 1910). But beyond fame, wealth and love he obviously wished to be regarded as an unprecedented technical virtuoso, a master of his craft. Beyond all the bravado and the support for unbridled hedonism, there was always a dedicated, professional side to Sinatra's personality, dedicated to the vocation of vocal perfectionism.

Patrimony

A little over ten years after he quit the Tommy Dorsey Orchestra in 1942 Sinatra commanded the patrimony that he felt was his due. He cut out the bandleader and the orchestra and became the unchallenged star. He was audacious, imperious, and narcissistic. Even in his cups, mourning the loss of Ava in the concept album *Only the Lonely* or engaging in savage onstage repartee, he portrays himself as residing above the common ruck, imparting wisdom rather than seeking it, providing a role model rather than supplicating one. Sinatra's legendary status was not founded on being liked more than other performers. His audience frequently disapproved of his behavior. In particular they regarded his Rat Pack insolence and his post–Rat Pack incarnation as "chairman of the board" as intimidating, his belligerence as coarse, his sexism as boorish, and his links with the Mafia as unsavory. Notwithstanding this, he became a legend for three reasons.

First, his comeback after 1953 was against all the odds and appealed to popular admiration for the national values, supposedly bolstered during the war, of courage and perseverance. Sinatra's Caesarism meant that he was usually capable of nothing more than false humility. His self-image was of a man possessed of unique talent and extraordinary achievement to whom automatic respect and deference was *de rigueur*. To be sure, in his personal behavior this was moderated and in some cases suspended with celebrities he had grown up with as a fan. Even in old age he was starstruck by Fred Astaire, Bing Crosby, Jimmy Durante, Humphrey Bogart, Spencer Tracy, and Edward G. Robinson. Nor was he beyond recognizing members of his own generations as worthy coevals, if not quite equals. Dean Martin, Robert Mitchum, Sammy Davis Jr, Count Basie and Nelson Riddle fall into this category. Significantly, after his comeback he also recognized belatedly, although never wholeheartedly, that there were public relations dangers attached to hauteur. In 1955 he appointed George Wood of the William Morris organization to be his agent. While his future career would hardly be free of scandal or public opprobrium, it never again descended into the prolonged public relations catastrophe of 1947–53.

Second, he embodied the collective sentiments of optimism and hedonism that flourished in America as consumer culture reinvented itself in the postwar period. Sinatra's public face of guiltless high living and unapologetic immediate gratification provided an antidote to those financially unleashed consumers who worried about abandoning thrift and restraint. He also offered carefree relief from public worries about the war in Korea, the Soviet threat, the atom bomb, and the unfolding national tragedy of Vietnam.

Third, his career reinforced and developed American myths of rugged individualism. To some extent American preeminence owed more to the legacy of adventurers, risk-takers and land-boomers than to the prim manners and orotund vocabulary of the founding fathers. Sinatra's links with organized crime, his defiance of convention, and his bellicose histrionics against the press, rival entertainers and government officials appealed to the American tradition of adventurism. He disregarded the conventions of humility to the media and record companies, and scorned obedience to officialdom.

In middle age Sinatra became the apotheosis of cool.

The Kingmaker

Perhaps from Sinatra's standpoint success exonerated the imperious, self-aggrandizing, pugnacious traits in his personality. If he sought validation it was provided as early as the late 1950s by his close association with John F. Kennedy. Kennedy consorted with the Rat Pack, joining with them in drinking sessions and sexual escapades. Despite Sinatra's public reputation for violence and his links with organized crime, Kennedy invited Sinatra to play a prominent part in the 1960 presidential election campaign. Kennedy's choice of Sinatra to organize and host the gala celebrations for his presidency was arguably the apogee of Sinatra's career. For a man so closely attuned to the barometer of public recognition as Sinatra, it was a magnificent honor. The sociologist C. Wright Mills had written about the growing significance of the celebrity elite in American life and speculated on the emergence of interlocking linkages with the political and business elites (Mills 1956). Now Sinatra's involvement with Kennedy provided a textbook example.

At this time, nothing seemed to elude Sinatra's power. The cult of Caesarism that surrounded him in the Rat Pack and in the world of popular entertainment now thrust him into the role of political kingmaker. He relished a new element in his self-mythology: friend and confidante of the President and welcome guest at the White House. For Sinatra, who throughout his life dreamt of fulfilling the Sicilian ideal of being a *uomo di rispetto*, a "man of respect" whose presence is automatically revered by society and who by a glance, word or gesture settles problems, it was a priceless accolade.

One should note that Sinatra's involvement with the Democrats was of long standing. His mother had been a political activist for the party in Hoboken, and after he became famous, Sinatra engaged in fundraising and campaigning activities for Franklin D. Roosevelt and, with Ava Gardner, for Adlai Stevenson in his presidential contest with Eisenhower. But Kennedy's campaign and presidency signified a self-conscious break with the past. Of course, since the days of Andrew Jackson presidential candidates have appreciated the value of public relations and public performance. But few were as well equipped as Kennedy to *seduce* the public. Kennedy oozed youth, sexuality and glamour. His campaign called for enlarged public responsibilities in defeating poverty, want and ignorance at home and expanding liberty and progress abroad. It was a confident, proactive stance that contrasted with the conservative, reactionary policies of the Eisenhower years. Kennedy exploited it to devastating effect in his television debates with the Republican candidate Richard M. Nixon. In these exchanges Kennedy seemed assured and open about the direction of American domestic and foreign policy, while Nixon seemed hesitant and furtive. Kennedy was to make great play of being the first President born in the twentieth century. For Sinatra, there was not only a sincere identification with Kennedy's policies of extending civil rights, increasing state investment in underprivileged communities and improving education and health care, there was also a thrilling sense of his own generation coming to power.

For its part, the Kennedy camp – at this time – judged that the energy and glamour that Sinatra and the Rat Pack radiated would increase the perception of JFK as a natural winner.

Later, long after Kennedy's assassination, evidence of Sinatra's role in providing Kennedy with a string of lovers, most notably Judith Campbell Exner, who was also sexually involved with Sinatra and with Sam Giancana, the Chicago Mafia boss, would surface, greatly diminishing the reputation of all protagonists. For the moment, the inaugural gala event constituted the crowning achievement of Sinatra's career: the undisputed master of ceremonies at the court that would later enter American history as "Camelot."

But as the administration got under way, Robert Kennedy's assault on organized crime turned the Sinatra connection into a liability. In addition, Sinatra embarrassed the Kennedy camp by defiantly hiring Albert Maltz, the old, blacklisted screenwriter of *The House I Live In*, to write the screenplay for a film that he was set on making, *The Execution of Private Slovik*. The film concerned the story of the only American soldier in World War Two to be shot for desertion. Maltz was a controversial choice for the new project because he had served a prison sentence during the McCarthy era for refusing to say whether or not he was a Communist. Perhaps Sinatra believed that his power immunized him from the consequences of working with a blacklisted member of the McCarthy era. He certainly regarded the hiring of Maltz as an act of defiance against the proceedings of HUAC and the right-wing press that supported them. "Once they get the movies throttled," he declared, "how long will it be before the committee goes to work on freedom of the air? . . . If you make a pitch on a nationwide radio network for a square deal for the underdog, will they call you a commie?" (quoted in Weiner 1991: 266.) Be that as it may, the Kennedys realized that the implication that a member of their circle was consorting with a suspected Communist was potentially politically devastating. As a result of pressure from the White House Sinatra fired Maltz, but honorably paid him his full screenwriter's fee and aborted the project. But in the Kennedy camp his reputation as a loose cannon was now set in stone. Questions of Sinatra's political judgment and speculation about his links with the Mafia quickly revived.

The Californian White House

After the Maltz affair, Kennedy was more wary in his public and private relations with Sinatra. The relationship became strained and eventually disintegrated in a dramatic fashion. In 1962 the President planned a visit to Sinatra's Palm Springs home. Nothing could have been calculated to appeal more to Sinatra's self-image as a *uomo di rispetto* and a *uomo d'onore*, a man of honor. In his mind's eye, the seat of power was temporarily relocating from Washington to his Palm Springs home. He was exultant. He set about making truly epic renovations to the property in preparation for JFK's visit. For example, he added a banquet room with seating space for 40; two cottages were built to house Secret Service agents; a communications center was constructed; a concrete heliport was installed; a towering flagpole was erected flying the presidential seal; a Kennedy room was established and furnished with mementos, framed personal notes and photographs; and a brass plaque was affixed to a bedroom door commemorating an earlier (nonpresidential) visit with "John F. Kennedy Slept Here, November 6th and 7th, 1960."[5] It was typical of Sinatra's sense of self-importance, but also demonstrated the genuine largesse that he lavished upon friends, especially if they possessed influence. In the event, the effort and money were wasted. Kennedy's advisors prevailed upon him that it would be a political miscalculation to accept Sinatra's hospitality and the visit was abruptly canceled. To Sinatra's incredulity, Kennedy stayed at the estate of the known Republican performer Bing Crosby.

To a large extent, Kennedy's advisors were right. In the early 1960s the press was treating Sinatra's Mafia links as no longer speculative but transparent. In 1963 a visit by Sam Giancana to Sinatra's casino hotel, Cal-Neva Lodge, Lake Tahoe, contravened a public ruling of the Nevada Gaming Control Board. Sinatra was secretly filmed socializing with Giancana. During the subsequent Gaming Control Board enquiry, despite his attempts to dismiss the episode as harmless fun, Sinatra's license was revoked and he was instructed to divest himself of his interests in the Cal-Neva and Sands casinos. Sinatra was livid and again resorted to the argument that he was a victim of establishment racism. Under sufferance, and with bad grace, he sold his casino interests. Sinatra shared the traditional Sicilian mistrust of officialdom and state interference in private matters. He regarded the judgment of the Nevada Gaming Control Board to be not only unjust but also an affront to his honor. In his mind, and in actuality, he had made an immense contribution to the wealth of the state through his performances in Las Vegas. For him, it followed that he deserved sympathy and respect from the authorities. Instead he received condescension and harassment.

The tendency to independently and automatically defend and avenge any violation of integrity to himself, his property or his family and friends recurs throughout Sinatra's career. It is evident in his disturbing acts of physical violence and litigation against journalists or others he believed did not treat him with sufficient respect. In his eyes, material success was never enough. The quest for power was all. He wanted to be viewed as a respectable member of the legitimate community – a figure whose activity is regarded as not simply a matter of self-interest, but mutual benefit. This is why he was magnetized by politics. Politics is the art of solving problems, achieving personal honor, and contributing to the common good. The leader who brings people together, solves problems and brings prosperity is the ultimate *uomo di rispetto* in the public sphere. For this reason he is also the key figure of influence in the power structure.

Padrone Reagan

When Sinatra's thoughts turned to making a serious attempt to regain his gambling license he approached President Reagan. But not before using his own influence to assist Reagan on the road to the White House and by this means, crucially, establishing an adhesive principle of reciprocity. Sinatra's drift to the

Republican Party began in the late 1960s. He was never part of Lyndon B. Johnson's circle. As president after John F. Kennedy's assassination, Johnson followed Robert Kennedy's position in regarding Sinatra as a mafioso and an electoral liability. Nor did Sinatra fare better with Johnson's Democrat successors. His offers to campaign and fundraise for Hubert Humphrey in the 1968 presidential contest with Richard Nixon foundered when the *Wall Street Journal* resuscitated allegations of Sinatra's links with organized crime. Humphrey was petitioned by his advisors to shun Sinatra, which he duly did. By then, Sinatra's move away from the Democrats was arguably more than a matter of hurt pride. It was motivated by the perception, shared with many voters, that "soft" solutions to crime, education, welfare and the economy had failed.

In the early 1960s Sinatra was openly dismissive of Ronald Reagan's campaign for the governorship of California. In fact, he denounced him as "a stupid bore who couldn't get into pictures" (Freedland 1997: 347). He was ostentatious in his scorn when Reagan was duly elected in 1966. But he backed Reagan in his successful campaign for reelection as Governor in 1970. At this time, Sinatra was not alone in regarding Reagan as an improbable candidate for President. Instead he backed Spiro T. Agnew, Nixon's Vice President. However, when Agnew resigned from office in ignominy in 1973 following revelations about tax evasion, Reagan's star gradually began to rise, both within the Republican Party and with Sinatra. Sinatra supported Reagan's campaign to be elected as President in 1980. Perhaps he also judged that Reagan's origins in show business would make him more sympathetic to Sinatra's difficulties with the Nevada Gaming Control Board. Be that as it may, Sinatra agreed to become involved in campaigning and fundraising for the Reagan campaign, a decision that eventually contributed $4 million to Republican coffers. Sinatra's fundraising role and public support was highly valued by the presidential candidate. Indeed, Nancy Reagan's praise was so fulsome that it triggered lewd media speculation that she was involved in a secret affair with Sinatra. There is no evidence to confirm the speculation. However, in a symbolic volte-face of his crowning moment at

Kennedy's inauguration in 1961, Sinatra organized the 1981 inaugural gala for the Republican Reagan, famously regaling Nancy with a revised, sycophantic version of his old nightclub standard, "Nancy (with the Laughing Face)."

Sinatra had delivered.

Reagan was now the *padrone* of American politics. In the psychology of the *uomo di rispetto*, the successful use of influence is an occasion for joy but also for the acknowledgment of reciprocity by those to whom favor has been granted. Sinatra was in no position to coerce Reagan to act on his behalf. On the other hand, by successfully assisting Reagan's path to the White House he established a precedent for reciprocity.

In 1981 Sinatra launched a legal challenge to reverse the judgment of the Nevada Gaming Control Board. He and his legal team solicited personal statements in Sinatra's favor from the great and the good in Hollywood. Kirk Douglas, Bob Hope and Gregory Peck provided sworn affidavits testifying to Sinatra's generosity and benevolence. A Catholic priest and friend of the Sinatra family, Father Herbert Ward, swore Sinatra to be God-fearing and trustworthy. Sinatra's friend Sheriff Peter Pitchess of Los Angeles County poured derision on the suggestion that Sinatra was a member of the Mafia. But arguably, it was President Ronald Reagan's letter of recommendation to the Nevada Gaming Control Board that represented Sinatra as "honorable," "loyal" and "completely honest" that proved decisive. The investigations of the Nevada Gaming Control Board found in Sinatra's favor, and awarded him back his gaming license.

In many respects it was a pyrrhic victory. To some extent, Sinatra's sense of outrage and smouldering injustice at the decision to relieve him of the Cal-Neva lodge and his investment in the Sands was appeased. But by 1981 the 66-year-old Sinatra was deep into the longest swansong in postwar American entertainment. Actually, he announced his retirement as early as 1971. The "last" concert in Los Angeles concluded with *Angel Eyes*, with its apt final refrain, "Scuse me while I disappear." But this, as with so much about the public face of Sinatra, was merely cosmetic.

The Final Curtain

Caesar cannot leave the people. He is bound to them by an umbilical cord, because they are the ultimate source of his power and sense of self-worth. Without the renewal of this popular connection his charisma declines. The accolades of other leaders and the honors given by states are as nothing compared to the tribute of the people. So it is with achieved celebrities. They often experience retirement as a vacuum because it affords no meaningful basis for the public replenishment of their honor and respect. This is why so many achieved celebrities continue working into their seventies, eighties and beyond, despite having no financial need to do so.

Sinatra recommenced touring in 1973 and continued until failing health forced him to abandon the stage in 1995. Some performances repeated the authority, insouciance and style that Sinatra radiated at his peak. In these concerts Sinatra seemed to defy the years. His voice had changed. The youthful light baritone with a two octave range from G to G darkened in later years, to what F. Balliett referred to "a Hoboken *bel canto* quality" (1998: 13). Nonetheless, the consummate power and confidence of the Rat Pack era and his famous performances with the Count Basie Orchestra in the 1960s were tangible. As I have already observed, age did not mellow him. He continued to defy controversy and to swim against the tide of political correctness. In 1981 his decision to agree to a ten-day engagement in Sun City, the playground for South African whites,[6] was widely condemned by blacks and the liberal press for colluding with apartheid. Conversely, he was also honored by others as a twentieth-century humanitarian, gaining the Medal of Freedom in 1985 and a Life Achievement Award from the Los Angeles branch of the National Association for the Advancement of Colored People in 1987.

In other concert performances Sinatra showed his age. Friedwald quotes Sinatra's piano accompanist Vincent Falcone, who ventured that by the early 1970s Sinatra's voice had deteriorated irreparably (Friedwald 1996: 487). Randall Taraborrelli submits that by the 1980s Sinatra's voice was already "ravaged" not simply by the ageing process but by his "careless lifestyle" (1997: 583). However, Sinatra partially disguised the decline by strenuous vocal exercises consisting of scales and arpeggios. He appears to have relaxed this regime somewhat in the 1980s, but by then his general health was becoming uncertain. In 1986 he collapsed on stage in Atlantic City and was officially diagnosed as suffering from diverticulitis. His doctors removed 12 inches of intestine and temporarily inserted a colostomy bag – horribly demeaning for the apotheosis of cool – prompting speculation that Sinatra was actually suffering from colon cancer. Sinatra was 71 at that time and was working five months a year with approximately 70 concert bookings. After he recovered, he returned to the stage and for a time reduced his pattern of bookings. Even so, in 1990 the 75-year-old Sinatra played 65 dates, he played 73 in 1991 and 84 in 1992. He still regarded himself as a global entertainer, performing in 17 different countries in 1991, including Australia, Ireland, Japan, and Sweden.

However, by the late 1980s and early 1990s his disabilities were abundantly evident. It was not just a question of his vocal powers. His memory was unreliable and he grew more dependent on autocues. In 1991 he was advised that he required a hearing aid in his left ear, and in 1993 he underwent two operations for the removal of cataracts in his eyes. In 1994 in Richmond, Virginia, he again collapsed on stage and was carried off in a wheelchair. Tina, his daughter, recalled that in an appearance at the Riviera Sinatra forgot the lyrics to one of his standards, *The Second Time Around*, and was bailed out by his audience finishing it for him (T. Sinatra 2000: 229). By the 1990s his performances were rarely triumphant, usually a pale shadow of his golden years and occasionally embarrassing. The press speculated that he was suffering from the onset of dementia, a proposition that became more frequent after his retirement. His final concert occurred in February 1995 at the Marriot Desert Springs Resort and Spa.

In his last decade as a public performer Sinatra was arguably more of a spectacle than an entertainer. Critics put his voice at three-fifths of its 1950s authority and power (Freedland

1997: 417). This was more than sufficient to deliver many memorable performances. But it was insufficient to guarantee consistency. Sinatra often faltered, failed to reach the correct notes, muffled his enunciation, and generally lost his way. But his presence as a legend symbolizing over half a century of achievement in popular music, film and celebrity lifestyle was enough to inspire popular homage. In his bow tie, white shirt and tuxedo he was an immortal icon of twentieth-century popular culture whose evident frailty oddly echoed the external vulnerability that was such a pronounced feature of his public face in the late 1930s and early 1940s. Sinatra spent all three ages of man – youth, middle age, and old age – in the spotlight. If the core of his fame was founded in the invulnerable, insouciant persona cultivated in middle age, the beginning and end of his career are united in the admittedly calculated, but nonetheless affecting, exhibition of human frailty.

Of course, in his later years Sinatra was uncomfortable about being regarded as a remnant of the past rather than a still vital and creative artist. He had feared ageing and death all his life and any insinuation that his powers of performance were receding was met with short shrift. He also affected a public humility that had not been seen since the days of *The House I Live In*. On the *Larry King Show* he dismissed the suggestion that he was preeminently famous for being a legend with what, by Sinatra's lights, was almost humility:

> I don't know what a legend means, I really don't quite understand. I'm not a stupid man, but the definition of legend is so broad, I don't know what it means. King Arthur was a legend, Franklin Roosevelt was a legend, and this guy, that guy...But what does it mean? It's longevity. I think if you're around long enough people become aware, your name comes up in conversation, people write about you. Your name comes up. (Taraborrelli 1997: 585)

This has more than a whiff of insincerity about it. The *uomo di rispetto* maneuvers himself to head a network of power and influence which awards him respect and veneration by dint of his position. It is a symbolic power that resorts to physical force only as a last resort. But it is consciously engineered and ferociously defended. The *uomo di rispetto* does not stoop to self-promotion in public. His influence in the community derives from being automatically acknowledged and revered as a leader and man of influence. So it is with a legendary celebrity. Sinatra knew his worth in American popular culture and he was quick to avenge any slight upon his reputation by threats, intimidation and litigation. In his later years his patient, determined efforts to regain his Nevada gambling license, and his acceptance of a variety of honorific medals and awards do not suggest the sudden blooming of a shrinking violet.

Sinatra was one of only a handful of iconic achieved celebrities in the popular culture of the twentieth century who created a personal mythology and body of work that defined not a single decade but over half of the century. He was "the Voice" of the 1940s, the leader of the Rat Pack and "chairman of the board" of the 1950s and 1960s, and "Ol' Blue Eyes" of the 1970s, 1980s and 1990s. As a pop idol of the 1940s, Sinatra was grafted into film early in his career. *Higher and Higher* (1943), *Anchors Away* (1945) and *It Happened in Brooklyn* (1947) required him to perform relatively undemanding roles for a captive, adoring teenage audience. These were unobjectionable and unremarkable films designed to achieve crossover capitalization from popular music to mass market film. He might have persisted with them – as, depressingly, Elvis Presley was to do at the behest of his avaricious manager, Colonel Tom Parker, in the 1960s. But in the 1950s Sinatra chose more challenging roles that addressed the dark side of American popular culture. *From Here to Eternity* explored class conflict and the politics of victimization; *Suddenly* (1954) – a neglected gem in the Sinatra film canon – deals with a plot to kill the President; *The Man with the Golden Arm* examined the transgressive world of heroin addiction; *The Joker Is Wild* was a biopic of Joe E. Lewis, a nightclub singer forced to change career after a rival club owner ordered assailants to cut his vocal chords. In the 1960s *The Manchurian Candidate* was based on Richard Condon's novel of a Congressional Medal of Honor war veteran who is brainwashed by the

Koreans to assassinate the President; the Tony Rome films (*Tony Rome*, 1967; *Lady in Cement*, 1968) focused on a hard-boiled Chandleresque detective loner.

These films dealt with the themes of the arid fantasies of Cold War American ideology, social friction, violence, alienation, and isolation. They demonstrate Sinatra's urge to make relevant, challenging films as a counterpoint to his straightforward mass market, money-making vehicles such as *Guys and Dolls* (1955), *The Tender Trap* (1955), *Can-Can* (1960), and the Rat Pack romps, of the 1960s, *Ocean's Eleven Sergeants Three, Four for Texas*, and *Robin and the Seven Hoods*.

Nor did Sinatra's recordings simply address carefree hedonism. He alternated up-tempo, escapist albums like *Songs for Swingin' Lovers, Come Fly with Me* and *Sinatra Swings* with *In the Wee Small Hours, Where Are You?, Only the Lonely* and *No One Cares*, which dealt piquantly with themes of rejection, loss, and emotional disintegration.

Sinatra's enormous fame derived not merely from his creative achievements in music and film but also from the persona and style of living that he cultivated. His public face transmitted assurance, boldness, confidence, insouciance and, perhaps above all, power. In the 1950s he personified the carefree hedonism of American consumer culture. As America's military and political role in the world expanded in Eastern Europe, Korea, Indo-China and, fatefully, into Vietnam, American popular culture grew more introspective and materialistic. Sinatra and the Rat Pack represented an idealized middle aged, male world of fooling around, gambling, leisurely rounds of golf, packed wallets, well-stocked drinks cabinets, and endless girlfriends offering sex without commitment. It was a world so self-centered and indifferent to global political and cultural realities that it bordered on the delusional. Conversely, so winning was this portrayal of carefree masculine West Coast hedonism that it overshadows Sinatra's unquestionable achievement in addressing abandonment, rejection, and emotional abuse. He was never a one-dimensional artist. His work took risks and, especially in the 1950s and 1960s, sought to change cultural attitudes.

Yet his career also illustrates the tensions of changing masculinity, the contradictions of American cultural imperialism, the shallowness of consumer culture, and the use of force and political influence to achieve goals. Sinatra was a brilliant success, but he was also the victim of cultural transformations that he did not fully understand. The loosening of puritan, white, Anglo-Saxon authoritarian values is something that his career helped to achieve. But in the final two decades of his life he clearly believed that the liberalization of culture had gone too far. Likewise in these years American culture evidently demurred from some aspects of Sinatra's persona, notably his belligerence, narcissism, and association with organized crime. Throughout the 1970s and 1980s he was ritually subpoenaed to appear before state and Congressional commissions investigating the Mafia. He was never charged with criminal activity. Perhaps his immunity from prosecution owed much to his alleged links with the CIA. Notwithstanding this, the public requests to defend himself contributed to the public perception of him as a disreputable star which all of his sterling work for charity, especially children's causes, failed to dissipate. As he struggled to remember the lines of songs on stage, with a cigarette in one hand and a glass of Jack Daniels in the other, he came to symptomatize an old-fashioned type of heroic, independent self-centered masculinity that was no longer acceptable in American life.

Nevertheless, Sinatra's presence in the landscape of postwar popular culture was sufficiently immense for him to thrive and prosper. More people revered him as a legend than cursed him as a tyrant and dissembler. Indeed, in his final years he had the uncanny experience for a living achieved celebrity of already being recognized as immortal.

---

two ---

UOMO DI RISPETTO

Sinatra died on May 14, 1998. In the UK the *Today* breakfast program on BBC Radio 4 broadcast the news with unseemly nonchalance. Sinatra had been in declining health for some time and his death was not unexpected. The program reported that the last word he uttered was "Mother"! If true, it is entirely apt. Dolly Sinatra was a titanic presence in Sinatra's life. On occasion, as he was wont to observe ruefully, she could be an ogre. In biographies of Sinatra she is variously described as "pushy," "foul-mouthed," "profane," "strenuous," "capable of great love," "hectoring," and "a small-time gangster" (Clarke 1997: 12, 23, 25; Kelley 1986: 3, 17; Freedland 1997: 14; Lahr 1998: 13; Taraborrelli 1997: 21).

Natalie Della Garavante's family emigrated to Hoboken from Genoa in the northwest of Italy. Dolly gained employment as a midwife and worked part-time as a chocolate dipper in a candy factory. To his great embarrassment, Kitty Kelley's unauthorized biography of Sinatra in 1986 highlighted Dolly's other career as a part-time abortionist. She was convicted of the offense in 1937. For the day it was not unusual for immigrant communities to have older women "helpers" to deal with unwanted pregnancies. Immigrants preferred folk medicine to legitimate doctors. Folk practice was generally free of condescension or moral disapproval and was delivered in a language that the patient could understand. It should also be emphasized that in Italian Catholic communities, unmarried women who became pregnant invited social censure and ostracism. Dolly, an arch pragmatist if ever there was one, saw her role as fulfilling a self-evident social need. She considered the law to be sanctimonious in respect of illegitimate pregnancy, and official medical provision to be inadequate. Sinatra was deeply ashamed about this part of her life. However, she is widely remembered as a "good" woman by many in the Italian Hoboken community, a woman who tried to provide practical solutions to people's problems where other routes were obstructed by red tape.[1]

Additionally, Dolly was a vigorous activist for the Italian-American community, agitating for City Hall to solve unemployment problems, control crime, and provide adequate public services. Such an interest in community life often culminates in political aspirations. To be sure, Dolly eventually became the Democrat leader of the third ward in Hoboken's ninth district. In the male-dominated, white Anglo Saxon culture that characterized American national and local politics of the day, this was an exceptional achievement. Dolly was the first Italian immigrant to hold such a post and almost certainly the first woman to do so (Clarke 1997: 10).

If Dolly was a titan in Sinatra's life, his father was a more diffident influence. The child of Frank and Rose Sinestro, grape-growers from Catania, Sicily, Anthony Martin Sinestro ("Marty") never learned to read or write. He provided Sinatra with a show-biz background of sorts, having fought over 30 professional boxing fights under the name "Marty O'Brien." The alias was chosen to appeal to the Irish population, which in demographic, political and economic terms dominated Hoboken. Marty abandoned boxing after fracturing his wrist and found work as a boilermaker in a shipyard. Dolly eventually pressured town officials into employing him as a fireman. He was appointed in 1927 and rose to the rank of captain without ever taking a written exam.

The Sinatras were an upwardly mobile family. After Frank's birth in 1915, they moved to successively larger houses in better neighborhoods. Later in life, Sinatra would regularly ventilate about the climate of racism and economic hardship that the Italian community suffered in Hoboken during his youth. The truth is that his family background was actually quite comfortable. For example, he held a private charge account and his fondness for fashionable clothes, especially slacks, earned him the nickname "Slacksie O'Brien."

However, if his parents thrived, they partly did so by operating on the fringes of legality. During the Prohibition era, 1919–33, they ran a tavern called Marty O'Brien's. The Volstead Act of 1919 outlawed the manufacture, transportation and sale of liquor, with the goal of achieving universal abstinence in the US. Judged as an effective piece of legislation, the Volstead Act fell at the hurdle because it invited a black market in liquor. Most historians consider it to have been misconceived and ineffectual. From the beginning it was ignored by many sections of the American public for whom the consumption of alcohol was an ineradicable part of culture. The police were left in an impossible situation. In areas where antagonism to the law was intense, the authorities bowed to public pressure and adopted a soft policing regime. Hoboken was one region of pragmatic policing in which orderly, comparatively discreet drinking places, like Marty O'Brien's, were permitted to trade unmolested. As a result, the Sinatras' business thrived. Prohibition also created new business opportunities in the illegal manufacture, sale and transportation of alcohol. This generated vast revenues for the Mafia and urban gangs. The Mafia supported an enormous twilight world of suppliers, transport workers, protection staff, and bootleggers.

Although criminal activity was obviously frowned upon in the Italian-American community, many held an ambivalent view of the Mafia. The folk prestige of the Mafia rested on three columns. First, in racially divided settler communities like Hoboken, many preferred the Mafia as a source of law enforcement to the police. The Mafia was Italian and obeyed a time-worn code of honor. The New Jersey police included representatives from ethnic minorities who were often hostile to Italian interests. For many Italian immigrants in New Jersey the devil you knew was preferable to entering the uncharted waters of po-faced American officialdom.

Second, the Mafia code of masculinity consecrated values of heroism and solidarity. In the 1920s and 1930s, for young Italian males like Sinatra who were victims of racial harassment, the Mafia offered an enormous resource of male racial defiance and pride. This was symbolized above all in the notorious Castellammarese wars where the Mafia took on the police and appeared to win.

Third, Mafia wealth and influence fulfilled the immigrant dream of abandoning the privations of the old country and achieving the good life. Although the methods used by the Mafia were unlicensed crime, they demonstrated the practical opportunities of rapid upward mobility offered in the American melting pot.

The Castellammarese Wars and their Aftermath

The Castellammarese wars (1930–1) among the Italian Mafia in New York provided a notorious backdrop to Sinatra's adolescence and supplied him with an enduring fund of popular images of Italian-American boldness, righteous enmity, and ineffable cool. Mafia stereotypes were glamorized in the Hollywood gangster films of the 1930s. According to Shaw (1968: 18), two of Sinatra's great movie heroes were Paul Muni (*Scarface*) and Edward G. Robinson (*Little Caesar*). In order to understand Sinatra's own attitude to masculinity, achievement and celebrity it is worth going into some basic details of the conflict.

By 1930 the criminal underworld was ruled from the Lower East Side by a Sicilian immigrant, Joe Masseria, and his lieutenants, Frank Costello, Albert Anastasia, Carlo Gambino, and Lucky Luciano. Masseria was not a popular leader. When Mussolini had begun to force Italian gang leaders into exile in the late 1920s, many had gravitated to New York. Most of them hailed from the region around the Bay of Castellammare, including Joseph Bonanno and Joe Profaci. The leader of this new wave of Mafia immigrants was Salvatore Maranzano. Maranzano established his headquarters in an office block near Grand Central Station and commenced to raid Joe "the Boss" Masseria's territory. The result was the infamous Castellammarese wars in which gang warfare erupted on the streets of New York.

In 1931 Masseria was murdered in Brooklyn by a team of his own lieutenants, including Ben Siegel, Albert Anastasia, Joe Adonis, and Red Levine, headed by Lucky Luciano. Maranzano rewarded Luciano by appointing him his second in command. Declaring himself the unchallenged victor of the Castellammarese wars, Maranzano set about establishing a blueprint for the *uomo nuovo* of Mafia rule in America. The Italian underworld would henceforth be divided into five criminal families. Each family was to be headed by a boss entitled to a tribute, a percentage of earnings from the "soldiers," the low-level members of the family. In return the soldiers were guaranteed protection from other criminals and the police by the praetorian guard of the Mafia. If a member of one family suffered wrong at the hands of a member of another, he was entitled to bring the matter to the attention of the family lieutenant, the *capo*, who would judge if the action required that the boss should be advised. In this event the boss had the right to decide if negotiation was required with the relevant boss from one of the other four crime families.

Maranzano's blueprint was intended to minimize warfare by creating clear territories and boundaries of criminal activity, with mutually agreed lines of arbitration and conciliation. In addition, soldiers were provided with insurance protection in the form of an impregnable guarantee that arrest on family business would require the family to fix bail, appoint a lawyer, and attempt to bribe the judge. In the event of criminal sentencing, the soldier's wife and children would be provided for by the boss. It was a system that sought to maximize solidarity and fasten automatic loyalty to the common criminal cause. The five families created by Maranzano were the Lucky Luciano family, the Albert Anastasia family, the Tommy Luchese family, the Joseph Profaci family and the Joseph Bonanno family. Their business operations were based in restaurants, gun-running, stores, bakeries, trucking companies, hotels, resorts, narcotics, and prostitution.

Although the structure made important concessions to the situation of industrial America, it was basically a neo-European model of criminal feudal fiefdoms ultimately responsible to a single leader: Maranzano, the *capo di tutti capi,* the boss of bosses. Succession was not based on the primogeniture system of blood-line. Rather, it obeyed principles of achievement, with power passing on to the most able or forceful lieutenant. For example, when Albert Anastasia was murdered in a midtown barbershop, his family became the Carlo Gambino family, which was eventually controlled by John Gotti. Sinatra had well-documented relations with the Gambino family, which I shall take up in more detail later. When Lucky Luciano was deported to Naples, his family became the Frank Costello family, then the Vito Genovese family, and then again, after Genovese fled to Sicily to avoid a charge of murder, the Frank Costello family. In short, Maranzano's structure aimed to put an end to open warfare in the ranks of the Mafia and established an ethic of cooperation that informed Mafia activity in the US for decades.

But, it was based on a fatal flaw.

Although Maranzano divided power between the five families he reserved for himself the status of *capo di tutti capi,* boss of bosses. Maranzano was aware that this invited a battle for succession. He judged Lucky Luciano to be the leading contender among the family bosses. This is why he appointed him as his chief lieutenant. By doing so he believed he could bind Luciano to his cause. From Luciano's perspective, the role was a poisoned chalice. It rewarded him with privileges denied to the other four family bosses. But by dint of this, it created a motive for other bosses to seek to depose him. It also meant that Maranzano knew exactly where Luciano was should the need arise to eliminate him.

In the summer of 1931 a seemingly trivial dispute in one of the leading garment unions, the Amalgamated Clothing Workers, led to the unraveling of the whole elaborate structure. The dispute created divisions between leading figures in the union. One faction, headed by Phil Orlofsky, turned to the gangster Louis Lepke, who supplied protection. The other faction, led by Sidney Hillman, turned for help to Lucky Luciano. Luciano refused to get involved on the grounds that Lepke possessed jurisdiction over Orlofsky. In desperation, Hillman contacted Maranzano, who proved more amenable. Maranzano's men intervened in the dispute, killing some of Lepke's "soldiers" and delivering the *coup de grace* to the structure of mutual reciprocity. Maranzano's compact was exposed as resting on a bed of sand.

When Maranzano instructed Luciano to visit him at his office on September 10, 1931, Luciano already knew of the plot to get rid of him. Tommy Luchese, a Maranzano confidante who was secretly in the employ of Luciano, leaked that Maranzano had prepared a death list of key Mafia personnel, including Luciano, Costello, Genovese, Willie Moretti, Joe Adonis, Dutch Schultz, and Al Capone. Maranzano's motive was to consolidate power by eliminating contenders. He delegated the Irish hitman, Vincent "Mad Dog" Coll to murder Luciano, Costello and Genovese that afternoon. Luciano had prepared his own counterplan with his lieutenant Meyer Lansky and immediately set it in motion. A team of gunmen, assembled by Lansky and posing as federal alcohol agents, raided Maranzano's Manhattan headquarters, forced entry into his office, and murdered him.

From this bloody confrontation a new gangland structure emerged that proved to have longevity. The position of *capo di tutti capi* was formally abolished; although, as in all fundamentally competitive structures, there were latent pressures in the system for one boss to aim for ascendancy over the others. For example, the 1947 summit of Mafia bosses in Havana that Sinatra attended was partly engineered to allow Lucky Luciano to claim de facto leadership. However, after the assassination of Maranzano, on a day to day basis the Mafia was now to be run like a business corporation.

The influence of Meyer Lansky in fashioning this new vision was vital. He was the authentic *uomo nuovo*, the man of imagination who sought to Americanize the Mafia from the fetters of an old-style European territorial and baronial gangland structure constrained by mechanical rituals of feuding and ultimately fruitless displays of honor. The future would be Mafia Inc. – ruled by the bosses who now constituted a board of directors rather than heads of families. Mafia Inc. was popularly known as "the Mob" or "the Syndicate." It was responsible for the key

decisions of criminal business management, including the determination of matters of life over death. Board members resolved
strategy and policy on the principle of one man one vote.
Implementation of executive decisions was outsourced by the
board to contract killers. The logic here was that killings attrib-
utable to third parties were less actionable by the authorities
than staff killings. Not that Mob personnel were excused from
executions when circumstances demanded. But in most cases
they were enacted by professional hitmen operating as clients of
the Mafia.

These cultural features permeated Sinatra's habitus, the
ethnic, immigrant mores, presuppositions and convictions
from which he emerged and which he faithfully represented in
later life. For a Hoboken-born Italian-American youth who was
used to routine racial harassment from Irish and German immigrants, and also the police, the Mafia underworld offered an
exotic model of manly courage, glamour, and worldly success.
Gangsters like Abe Reles, Bugsy Siegel and Lucky Luciano lived
in sought-after apartments, wore the best suits, had the most
beautiful women, and superficially were the very embodiment
of the male American dream. If many Italian immigrants and
Italian-Americans disapproved of them and despised their
machismo, others glorified them as folk heroes, renewing
pride and honor in a diaspora that habitually suffered the brick-
bats of WASP condescension, and racial violence at the hands of
other ethnic minorities. The flamboyance and largesse of many
Mafia leaders was a direct response to public popularity. For
example, Reles was known to be an immoderate tipper. He
would regularly give newspaper sellers a $50 bill for a 50 cent
paper and tell them to keep the change. It was a form of protection and it enhanced the myth of Mafia personnel as folk heroes.
Reles justified his generosity by stating that he was "investing in
my legend."

Interestingly, among hotel and restaurant staff Sinatra was
also renowned as an extremely generous tipper. In his later
years, his evening routine when in Manhattan was to start at
Sardi's, stop at Jilly's, move on to Jimmy Weston's, Mike
Manuche's and end at P. J. Clarke's where he "owned" table

20. Sinatra would generally leave a hefty tip at each venue, although rarely as big as the $200 he was rumored to give room attendants and bellboys during his controversial tour of Australia in 1974.[2]

Many of Sinatra's traits that may be interpreted as reflecting his Italian-American background are also typical of standard Mafia practice. One thinks of his tendency toward tribalism, his practice of constructing intensely loyal male groups around him, of which the Rat Pack was the most public expression; his insistence on sartorial elegance; the cult of secrecy which he practiced, born out of a fierce, innate mistrust of both official-dom and the media; and his ready resort to intimidation and threats in disputes. Sinatra understood as well as any Maran-zano or Lucky Luciano that generosity carries obligations. The gift is an expression of beneficence, but it is also a basis for reciprocity. The male groups that he gathered around him acted as a buffer between him and the media and public, but they also constituted a network of reciprocity in which gifts dispensed by Sinatra could be used as the basis for "favors" when circumstances demanded.

If one thinks of everyday social exchanges as bounded by tacit rules, Sinatra thrived by the calculated pushing back of custom-ary boundaries, by working on the edge of socially agreed conventions to acquire advantage. This was also part of his habitus. Like most immigrants, Marty and Dolly Sinatra were opportunists in the land of opportunity. Both the tavern and "helping" women through unwanted pregnancies were illegal means to secure what they took to be the legitimate ends of material success and supplying social demand. From their standpoint, it was American WASP law, not their behavior, that was unreasonable. Competitive advantage lay in calculating when and how far to test legal conventions, with the precondi-tion of first having created a strategic network of indebtedness to act as both a protection policy and a basis for affirming reciprocity in the future. As immigrants, the Sinatras applied to America immemorial precepts and systems of patronage and clientism that had been tried and tested in Italy, and especially Sicily, for centuries.

Alta Italia and *Italia Bassa*

In terms of ethnic and honorific criteria the marriage between Marty and Dolly reflected deep asymmetries in Italian culture. Thus Dolly's family were trained lithographers who hailed from the more "advanced" north of Italy. Her background was of the "respectable" artisan class. She received elementary schooling, and from an early age appears to have had no scruples in combating officialdom. There is a confidence about her behavior as an immigrant in America that is less apparent in Sinatra's father. Marty's parents were peasant farmers from the "backward," "crimogenic" south of Italy. He was illiterate, and drifted into a career as a prizefighter – a typical lower class male strategy to acquire rapid upward mobility. When injury forced him out of the ring he fell back into unskilled blue-collar work, before Dolly intervened to secure him upward social mobility in the fire service.

The cultural and economic divisions between North and South run deep in Italian life and carry potent distinctions of ascribed status. The North is sometimes referred to as *alta Italia* (high Italy), an area that signifies discipline, sobriety, thrift, and industry. In contrast, the South is known as *Italia bassa* (low Italy), a region characterized by supposedly indolent, work-shy, criminal elements. The benchmark for this division in the South, especially in Sicily, is of course the Mafia.

Throughout his career Sinatra was dogged by media charges that he was in the service of the mob. Mafia intimidation was alleged to have forced Tommy Dorsey to free him from his financially punitive contract with the Tommy Dorsey Band in 1942. According to entertainment industry folklore, only the application of a pistol inside Dorsey's mouth finally persuaded him to release Sinatra. FBI reports include unconfirmed speculation that Sinatra paid Frank Costello $150,000 to harass Dorsey and, after being freed from his contract, was obligated to the Mafia to play engagements at the Copacabana nightclub in New York. In addition, Mafia death threats were alleged to have secured Sinatra the part of Private Maggio in *From Here to*

Eternity (1953), over Eli Wallach who was reported to have produced a superior screen test. Francis Ford Coppola's brilliant parable of Mafia, immigrant upward mobility in the US, *The Godfather* (1974), recalls the episode in the role of the Italian bobbysoxer idol Johnny Fontaine (played by Al Martino), who requests a "favor" from Don Corleone to secure a crucial screen role in a war movie. In the film the autocratic film producer only agrees to give Fontaine the role after the severed head of his champion racehorse is found in his bed. Interestingly, Coppola is understood to have wanted Sinatra for the part of Don Corleone. Be that as it may, speculation that the young Sinatra was the model for Johnny Fontaine is well established. But these innuendos are as of nothing, compared with the evidence of Sinatra's connections with the Mafia in the recently released FBI files.

The Mafia Code of Masculine Honor

Before examining the detailed FBI findings on Sinatra's involvement with the Mafia, it is important to turn to the question of the history and mythology of the Sicilian Mafia, especially the Mafia code of masculinity. The Hoboken in which the Sinatra family settled was not Main Street USA *à la* Disneyland or Disneyworld. Policing obviously existed in Hoboken. But there were also powerful territorial traditions of lawlessness and institutionalized racism in the immigrant districts. Sinatra was raised in a climate of racial abuse in which the most bellicose among the Irish and Germans regarded the Italians as nothing more than a race of white vermin. In youth culture this tradition of territorial racism fueled the eruption of violent gang cultures. The main youth gangs were segregated along racial lines, with the Irish, German and Italian elements ascendant. Like most Italian children of his generation, Sinatra was the occasional victim of gangland intimidation and violence. He certainly regarded himself at this time to be part of the "Italian-American neighborhood," and understood that physical and moral obligations follow the bloodline.

His heartfelt and lifelong detestation of racism has its origins in this period. As he put it: "In Hoboken when I was a kid...and somebody called me a 'dirty little Guinea,' there was only one thing to do – break his head. After I got older, I realized you've got to do it through education" (quoted in Shaw 1968: 88). When he took the role of the victimized Private Maggio from New Jersey in *From Here to Eternity* he observed, "I knew him...I was beaten up with him in Hoboken" (Shaw 1968: 16). In the racial pressure cooker of Hoboken in the 1920s and 1930s, the Mafia tradition of masculine violence, and to a lesser extent the Sicilian tradition of heroic banditry, provided compelling motifs for identity formation and symbolic cultural posturing. Sinatra did not have to be inducted by the Mafiosi to internalize their values and outlook. Rather they formed part of the resources of masculinity through which Italian male youth in Hoboken confronted their tribal gangland enemies.

What were the origins of this Mafia tradition of masculine violence? Why was Sinatra drawn to these old world traditions as he elevated himself as a show business tyro in twentieth-century American popular culture? The linchpins of masculine authority in the Sicilian Mafia are the values of arrogance, boldness, and solidarity. The *uomo d'onore*, the man of honor, acquires that honor through the accomplishment of particular *gesta* (feats). Murder and acquittal are the most prized *gesta*. More general methods are intimidation, fraud, bribery, extortion, and the fearless demonstration of personal freedom from the judicial institutions of officialdom. While Mafia power is often popularly associated with clandestine organization, it is in fact based in transparency. The power of the mafioso derives from the *automatic, unassailable* visible recognition of the voluntary renunciation of legal-rational interdictions and official moral prohibitions, and the use of self-licensed intimidation and violence to achieve ends. The doctrine of *omerta* equates respect with observing silence about *gesta* witnessed, committed, or endured. Reticence and secrecy, especially in relation to officialdom, are highly revered. As Blok observes (1974: 212), *omerta* acts as a form of social control since to ignore the doctrine directly challenges the position of the powerbroker. It brands as

Uomo di Rispetto

deplorable any man who turns to the police, judiciary or press to pursue his interest. By the same token, it dispenses mutual benefits to those who obey the doctrine, since dishonor shown to the bearer of *omerta* must ultimately be avenged by the power-broker. Revenge in respect of slights and deeds, real or imagined, is therefore woven into the Mafia power structure. The code of masculinity that derives from this outlook privileges independence, decisiveness and righteous vengeance in masculine action.

The power of the *uomo di rispetto* stems from the general recognition that he is superior to other men in acting independently and decisively to defend his honor and that of his family. The social structure of the Mafia is intensely competitive, with real and symbolic trials of strength playing a pivotal role in pronouncing dominance. In traditional Sicilian society, balls, festivals and pilgrimages provided public opportunities for both displaying an individual's personal strength and challenging the power hierarchy (Blok 1974; Arlacchi 1986). But armed struggle, bribery, fraud and assassination were also employed.

An important element in the prestige of the mafioso is the capacity to break the law with impunity. However, it is a mistake to regard the Mafia as an oppositional or revolutionary force in society. On the contrary, the mafioso exerts maximum influence when he is able to exercise control by co-opting individuals employed in the legitimate police, judiciary, business, and professions. The mafioso aims to establish a tutelage relationship with legitimate society in which "favors" are offered for demonstrations of loyalty and the collection of "tributes." Typically, the *uomo di rispetto*, man of respect, is committed to the preservation of order and the repression of nonconformist behavior, since these are the conditions which allow the Mafia to flourish unmolested.

Traditionally, the Mafia has shown low levels of tolerance to vagabonds, homosexuals, bandits, and revolutionaries. Often sentimental about the peasantry, mafiosi revile physical labor as inferior, as belonging to the benighted realm of *miseria*. The idealized male is the *gentiluomo*, free of the need to engage in manual labor, having abundant time and space for leisure, devoid of debt, with ample funds to devote himself to higher/ noble things.

The three preconditions of Mafia dominance are:

- *Preeminence* The demonstration of paramountcy in the competitive struggle to dominate the family and rival families.
- *Monopolization of a universal system of "favors" and "tributes"* Through the performance of *gesta* the Mafia demonstrates its ability to offer effective social protection in the community.
- *Mediation* The capacity to settle conflicts in the local setting and the world outside through the efficient mobilization of "influence."

The Mafia and Social Structure

The Mafia follows a masculine code of finding private solutions to social and economic problems and therefore bypassing the official conflict resolution mechanisms of the state. This is the corollary of a weakly integrated state that is unable to exercise cohesive power from the center. The undetermined character of centralized dynastic or bureaucratic-legal legitimate power creates the basis for decentralized fiefdoms that administer protection and private justice. The people of Sicily suffered a long history of domination by successive waves of foreign invaders. The Romans, Saracens, Arabs and Spanish successively conquered the island between the third and the eighteenth centuries. Arguably, until the 1920s when Mussolini's Fascist regime imposed ruthless repressive force – and incidentally came close to eradicating the Mafia as a power in Sicily – the region lacked an example of strong, centralized, enveloping control. The uneven interstices of colonial and dynastic power provided shelter for the Mafia to sprout forth and prosper.

The Mafia emerged in the late Middle Ages from the numerous small private armies, the *bravi*, hired by absentee landlords to protect their estates from brigands and bandits. From the spoils of these mercenaries developed independent groups capable of administering private justice in return for protection. They were never fully incorporated or controlled by the invading powers. Indeed, the invaders were typically forced to reach informal arrangements and reparation with them to maintain the peace by keeping bandits at bay. In 1487 Fra Antonio Della Penna was sent to Sicily by King Ferdinand of Spain to establish a secret network of *familiari* or collaborationists to monitor the religious faithful and fight heresy. In 1535 the *Familiari dell'Inquisizione* were ruled to be exempt from external jurisdiction, held their own courts, and contrary to the general prohibition, were permitted to bear arms. The unintentional consequence of this was to provide a fillip to the tradition of decentralized, clandestine private justice in Sicily, and thus to enhance the power of Mafia families.

Feudalism persisted in Sicily after the unification of Italy in 1861. The bureaucratic-legal state struggled to achieve legitimacy. In the hiatus of power between the 1860s and 1920s the Mafia gained competitive advantage. In many areas of Sicily and Calabria at this time, the mafioso acted as a proxy for the state, recruiting the personnel of the local police and advising on judicial, medical and clerical appointments. Tactically, the mafioso engineered various compromises with officialdom in order to acquire the mask of legitimacy. This was required for the long-term survival of Mafia power structures, especially in conditions where the power of the bureaucratic-legal state was growing. The Mafia's predilection for conniving with the representatives of formal law while disregarding the law through the administration of private justice distinguishes its specific form of organization from that of social bandits (Blok 1974: 94–5).

Eric Hobsbawm (1969) has emphasized the role of social banditry in articulating the craving for a new kind of society based on the end of injustice and suffering. He situates it in the context of the class tensions of capitalist society. While this heroic tradition was an element of the mythology of the bandit tradition in Sicily, its importance should not be exaggerated. Sicilian bandits were typically ad hoc groupings bent on achieving short-term revenge or opportunistic accumulation. Unlike the Mafia, they did not seek a qualified rapprochement with the state. One of the clearest examples of this rapprochement among the Mafia is the practice of political sponsorship. As Arlacchi puts it:

> Through the *mafioso*, a good many elements of local political life participated in the national political system. In pursuit of votes, the "system of notables" turned to the mafia for help in those areas immune to the usual electoral strategies. The mafia chief was almost always a major local elector, whose support was needed by any candidate for political or administrative office...
> In return for their support at elections – support guaranteed quite "legally" through the maintenance of clientelistic relations, as well as by means of threats, corruption and even sometimes the kidnapping of electors – government politicians granted favours to the *mafioso* and their associates: a gun-licence issued, a police report altered, an over-zealous official transferred elsewhere, the process of legal rehabilitation made smoother, and so on. (1986: 41)

The elective affinity between crime and legitimate politics became strongly pronounced in the organization and strategy of the Mafia at this time.

In the nineteenth and early twentieth centuries immigrants from Sicily with Mafia pedigrees or affiliations encountered relatively undetermined conditions of legitimate power broker-age in American cities bulging with new migrants. The state was unable to exercise either penetrating or binding policing of the territorially divided immigrant areas. In the Prohibition era, bootlegging provided a golden opportunity for fast money and the Mafia exploited it enthusiastically. After the repeal of Pro-hibition ended bootlegging in 1933, the Mafia diversified into gambling, labor racketeering, fraud, extortion, narcotics distri-bution, and prostitution. In the late 1940s and 1950s, as America embraced a culture of hedonism partly as an antidote to the anxieties of the Cold War, the development of gambling casinos and nightclubs in the West provided new business opportun-ities, in some of which Sinatra was at least a sleeping partner. FBI lists identified the Sands Casino and Cal-Neva lodge as

Mafia-sponsored operations. Sinatra held a substantial share-holding in both entertainment venues.

Kelley (1986: 295) contends that Sinatra himself was directly involved in the old Mafia game of political sponsorship and vote-rigging by "disbursing" Mafia money to pay off key election officials in the West Virginia primary during John F. Kennedy's election campaign. He is further alleged to have colluded with Sam Giancana and Skinny D'Amato to turn the coal miners' unions and other political organizations to support the Democrat cause. The accusations sit well with what is known about the standard practice of Mafia sponsorship of politicians and state officials. They also fit with what is known about Mafia diversification into the entertainment industry after 1933 (Denton and Morris 2002). However, the central impulse of Mafia organization remained the progressive accumulation of capacity for informal, clandestine physical force and economic might. Less is known about Sinatra's influence in this regard. In relation to allegations about Mafia links, Sinatra always presented himself as the victim of idle media speculation. But the extensive FBI files on Sinatra's alleged links with the Mafia, gathered over several decades, provide a basis for reassessing Sinatra's oft-repeated claim that the evidence linking him to the Mafia was strictly hearsay.

Sinatra and the Mafia

The FBI files present ample documentary evidence to confirm that Sinatra associated with members of the Mafia. Sinatra socialized with known linchpins in the Mafia; he is known to have performed on several occasions for Mafia gatherings; and he invested in known Mafia businesses. Belatedly, Tina Sinatra has sought to explain this as a reflection of Sinatra's steadfast identification with the Italian-American community:

> My dad grew up with gangsters next door. He was living with them. They were his personal friends, and he's not going to cast away a friend. The great vein through Frank Sinatra is loyalty.

Uomo di Rispetto

> There is an absolute commitment to friends and family. It's very
> Italian and probably gave him more than a little in common with
> mob types. (Quoted in Hersh 1998: 138)

This will not do. After all, not all Italian-Americans associate
with underworld figures. Jimmy Roselli, Sinatra's great rival for
the affection of the Italian-American community, refused to
become the court entertainer of Mafia bosses and his career
was damaged as a result. Dean Martin also rebuffed overtures
to become more involved with the Mafia. Moreover, the homely
picture of loyalty to friends that Tina Sinatra paints is obviously
questionable. For example, it did not extend to many of Sinatra's
other close friends who were either temporarily ostracized from
his circle, like Sammy Davis Jr, or summarily dumped, like
Lauren Bacall and Peter Lawford. We will come to the reasons
behind these conflicts in the next chapter.

Nor is Sinatra's own attempt at self-exculpation with regard to
the Mafia persuasive. Typically, he presented his links with
them as incidental and superficial. Thus:

> Did I know those guys? Sure, I knew some of those guys. I spent
> a lot of time working in saloons. And saloons are not run by the
> Christian Brothers. There were a lot of guys around, and they
> came out of Prohibition, and they ran pretty good saloons. I was a
> kid. I worked in the places that were open. They paid you, and
> the checks didn't bounce. I didn't meet any Nobel Prize winners
> in saloons. But if Francis of Assisi was a singer and worked in
> saloons, he would've met the same guys. That doesn't make him
> part of something. They said hello, you said hello. They came
> backstage. They thanked you. You offered them a drink. That
> was it. (Quoted in Hamill 1998: 146)

This is too glib. Sinatra cultivated his relationships with Mafia
figures, often in the face of severe public disquiet, for over half a
century. His relationships with them extend beyond friendship
to business ties. He relished their company, coveted their respect, and used his connections with them to add to his stature
as a man of respect in the show-business community.[3] He was
fascinated by their power and learned much from their practices

77

of bribery and intimidation. He respected their capacity to achieve immunity from prosecution and he approved of their contempt for officialdom. In his mind the links with the Mafia enhanced his legendary status and further marked him out as unique from other performers.

Arguably his association with the Mafia preceded his birth. His uncle Babe Garavante was connected to an underworld gang in Bergen County and northern New Jersey run by the gang leader Willie Moretti. As I have already noted, for many young male Italian-Americans the Mafia offered a role model of an exotic folk hero, whose unlicensed criminal activity was associated with excitement and wealth. The Sinatra family's involvement in the liquor trade inevitably connected them to this world. His uncles Champ and Lawrence Garavante were widely rumoured to have been arrested for bootlegging in Hoboken in the 1920s and early 1930s. However, no verification of this exists in the FBI files. In contrast, Babe Garavante unquestionably had a criminal record. In 1921 he received a sentence of 10–15 years hard labor and a fine of $1,000 as punishment for being the driver of a getaway car in an attempted robbery. The driver of a Railway Express Company truck was killed in the incident.

FBI files point to lifelong links between Sinatra and the Mafia. In the early 1940s he befriended Charles "Trigger Happy" Fischetti, a Mafia political fixer in Chicago. Sinatra is known to have socialized with Fischetti and obtained free tickets to sports events for him. He also made commercials for Fischetti's auto dealerships for free. FBI phone taps reveal significant and prolonged telephone contact between the two. Sinatra performed without charge at the Fountainebleau Hotel in Miami, in which Fischetti had a business interest. Fischetti is also alleged to have secured nightclub bookings for Sinatra at the nadir of his career between 1947 and 1953.

Nancy Barbato, Sinatra's first wife, was a cousin of one of Willie Moretti's lieutenants in the northern New Jersey Mafia. Moretti championed Sinatra in the 1940s, securing several concert bookings for him. Moretti's interest contributed to making Sinatra a cause célèbre for other Mafia leaders. By the late 1960s

Sinatra's concerts were regularly attended by leading mafiosi, including Santos Trafficante, boss of Florida, Carlos Marcello, boss of New Orleans, Frank Balistieri, boss of Milwaukee, and several members of the Gambino family in New York. In 1948, prefiguring the Johnny Fontaine scenes in *The Godfather*, Sinatra sang at the wedding of Moretti's daughter. He also performed for free at Skinny D'Amato's 500 Club in Atlantic City. D'Amato ran gambling and prostitution rackets, and helped Sinatra to secure nightclub bookings during the "Dark Ages." In 1962, D'Amato became a business partner with Sinatra in acquiring a controlling interest in the $4 million casino hotel, the Cal-Neva Lodge, Lake Tahoe (Williams 200: 102). Sinatra got 25 percent of the equity, Hank Sanicola, a sometime piano accompanist and business manager for Sinatra, got 16 percent, D'Amato 13 percent, and Dean Martin 3 percent.

Mickey Cohen, a lieutenant in Bugsy Siegel's organization on the West Coast fraternized with Sinatra. Sinatra visited him in 1948 to implore him to prevent Cohen's bodyguard Johnny Stompanato from seeing Ava Gardner.[4] Cohen refused to get involved. However, on at least one occasion he phoned Sinatra and asked him to meet a "business associate" from Ohio. Cohen also acted as the intermediary between Sinatra and James Tarantino, publisher of the risqué Hollywood news/rumour sheet *Hollywood Nite Life*. Tarantino used the publication to intimidate and blackmail movie stars. Sinatra was alleged to have invested $15,000 in starting the magazine.

Perhaps the most glamorous Italian gang leader of the 1920s and 1930s was Charles "Lucky" Luciano. He is estimated to have authorized over 500 murders and, with Meyer Lansky, to have controlled a multimillion-dollar criminal business. Sinatra is known to have performed for Lucky Luciano twice, the second occasion being the notorious gathering of the Mafia in Havana in 1947. At this meeting Sinatra was alleged to have carried a suitcase containing $2 million in cash as a tribute – an allegation that Sinatra always repudiated. Luciano was a notable antihero for many Italian-Americans of Sinatra's generation. He had outsmarted the dreaded officialdom that policed American society, and set new standards of cool, power and glamour for others to emulate. Luciano was eventually imprisoned and deported to Italy, ironically on trumped-up charges of pimping. Later, a police raid at his new home in Naples discovered a gold cigarette case that bore the inscription, "To my dear pal Lucky, From his friend Frank Sinatra."

Sinatra's singing rival in Hoboken, Jimmy Roselli, born a decade later, always disparaged Sinatra's readiness to perform gratis at Mafia functions. Sinatra is known to have performed for free at Mafia-controlled venues, notably at the 500 Club in Atlantic City run by Skinny D'Amato in the 1960s, and the Villa Venice near Chicago owned by Sam Giancana. During a week-long engagement at the 500 Club Sinatra hired a floor of Claridge's Hotel for guests of Angelo Bruno, the mob chief in Philadelphia, to celebrate the wedding of Bruno's daughter. For Jimmy Roselli, Sinatra possessed no scruples and would entertain Mafia bosses, play golf with them, and procure girls for them. Roselli's own career was damaged by his refusal to follow in Sinatra's footsteps. He lost nightclub bookings and his records were banned from WNEW-AM, New York's popular music radio station. Roselli suspected Sinatra's involvement:

> They used to play the hell out of my records. Sinatra must have said this guy moves too much or whatever. Of course it was Sinatra...Sinatra got jealous of me and it's not hearsay. I know. Because he was in the company of wiseguys and anytime he got in their company, my name came up. Because I was always the sweetheart of the wiseguys. If not them, their mothers, their wives. (Quoted in Evanier 2002: 170)

Roselli portrays Sinatra as the chosen entertainer of the Mafia, a man unencumbered by moral baggage:

> A guy like Frank, he jumped into bed with anybody. He don't give a fuck as long as his career went ahead. A friend of mine, a millionaire, one night he said to me, "I'd like to meet a couple of girls." I said, "Listen, I'm a singer, not a pimp. If you want to meet girls, I have nothing to do with that. I *sing*." But Frank, if he knew anybody he'd introduce you. I'm sure he was instrumental in Marilyn Monroe meeting Jack Kennedy. That in essence is a

pimp...For every little good thing [he] does, he does so much bad. So if you put it on a scale...Look, I don't even want to be in his company. Because I see how he acts. I see him at Jilly's [a nightclub]. He's hitting guys with cream pies, with ice cubes. He throws firecrackers, big bombs, under somebody's chair. He don't even know how to have fun, this guy...Much as he wanted to be a singer Sinatra would have given up his whole career to be a don. (Quoted in Evanier 2002: 229–30, 170, emphasis in original)

Interestingly, Bing Crosby was also reported as saying that "Sinatra always nurtured a secret desire to be a hood" (Shaw 1968: 18). Sinatra found the Mafia spirit of lawlessness, hubris and powers of intimidation irresistible. By the same token, Mafia bosses were beguiled by Sinatra's assurance and admired his loyalty. As Robert Buccino, the deputy chief investigator of the New Jersey division of the Criminal Justice, Organized Crime and Racketeering Bureau, observed:

For the Cosa Nostra, it was a badge of honour to be with entertainers and politicians. And the same with the entertainers: it was their moment of glory to be arm in arm with the Cosa Nostra... Sinatra was always there for them: if they asked him to do a charity, a casino, he did it. What really benefited him was that he showed loyalty to them. He never talked. (Quoted in Evanier 2002: 65)

Mr Giancana

Never was this truer than in respect of Sinatra's friendship with Sam Giancana. Giancana was a notorious underworld figure. He was rumored to be the driver and a gunman in the 1929 St Valentine's Day Massacre. By the late 1950s he was chief of the Chicago Mafia with interests in protection, pinball, prostitution, gambling, extortion, counterfeiting, and bookmaking. He was arrested over 70 times, on three occasions for murder. Giancana is thought to have ordered the deaths of over 200 people in his rule over a crime syndicate stretching from Chicago to Las

Vegas. Giancana's relationship with Sinatra is among the best documented on the FBI files. For this reason it is worth elucidating at some length.

In 1959 Sinatra testified to Internal Revenue Service (IRS) investigators that he met Giancana in 1958 and that relations between them were superficial. The affidavit on the issue reads thus:

Q: Are you acquainted with Mr. Sam Giancana?
A: I am.
Q: How long have you known the gentleman?
A: A couple of years. A little under a couple of years.
Q: Approximately, when did you first meet Mr. Giancana?
A: March 11, I think, 1958.
Q: Where did the meeting take place?
A: In the Fountainebleau Hotel.
Q: Miami Beach, Florida?
A: Yes.
Q: Have you ever had any business dealings with Mr. Giancana?
A: No.
Q: When was the last time you saw Mr Giancana?
A: Sometime early in August.
Q: 1959.
A: At the Chicago Airport, in 1959.
Q: Mr. Sinatra, in regard to the previous interview which we had with you on November 16, 1959, at your attorney's office, at that time you supplied information substantially as follows: That your relationship with Mr. Giancana was strictly friendly; that you had seen him approximately 6 to 10 times, several of these meetings having taken place at the Sands Hotel, Las Vegas, Nevada, where you were appearing at the time.
A: Yes.
Q: That you considered Mr. Giancana more or less a fan of yours; that you possess no knowledge as to Mr. Giancana's business activities; that you have never been approached by Mr. Giancana with a financial proposition. Is that correct?
A: That is absolutely correct.

Q: Do you have any way of knowing at this time how Mr. Giancana would have come into possession of your unpublished home phone number, CR 4-2368, listed to you at 2666 Bowmount Drive, Beverly Hills, California? Can you give us information as to how he may have come –

A: I gave it to him.

Q: Was there anything specific that you recall with reference to giving him this phone number?

A: Not at all. I give my phone number to many people.

Q: Would this likewise be true of your Crestview 5-4977, Oxford Publications Inc., the unpublished number, Texas 0-8701, your unpublished phone number at Metro Goldwyn Studios?

A: Yes.

Q: Was there any specific purpose that you had given these numbers to Mr. Giancana?

A: None.

Q: Mr. Sinatra, information has come to our attention that during the period July 25, 1959 to August 2, 1959, you were staying at the Hotel Claridge, Atlantic City, New Jersey, and at that time you had rented numerous rooms at this hotel and had given a party which was attended by Mr. Giancana. Is that correct?

A: No.

Q: Were you staying at the Claridge at this time?

A: Yes.

Q: Has Mr. Giancana attended any parties given by you, Mr. Sinatra?

A: No.

Q: With reference to the last interview, at that time you supplied information that the occasion of your last meeting with Mr. Giancana was in Chicago and at that time you had contacted Mr. Giancana for the purpose of making arrangements to have him transfer your luggage from the airport to the train in Chicago. Is that correct?

A: I guess so, except one little thing. I don't remember calling him because I don't know where to call him. Apparently – I have to guess, but apparently he called me; that is probably what happened. I don't remember calling him. I wouldn't know where to call him.

Q: Have you ever had occasion to visit Mr Giancana at his residence in Chicago?
A: No.
Q: Do you know where he lives?
A: No.

This facade of polite discretion crumbles when one looks at the facts. The FBI files unequivocally point to a closer relationship. Sinatra is known to have fraternized extensively with Giancana in Chicago and elsewhere. Peter Lawford chided Sinatra for "flaunting" his friendship with Giancana and alleged that the mafioso was "often" a guest at Rancho Mirage, Sinatra's Palm Springs estate (Schlesinger 1978: 495–6). Chuck Giancana described Sinatra's relationship with Sam as "deferential" and credited him with supplying compliant "broads too dumb to ask questions" in Vegas and elsewhere (Giancana and Giancana 1992: 357). When pressed about the nature of the relationship Sam Giancana is alleged to have said: "I'm his fuckin' hero. Frank is one of the few people I know who will follow through...the guy's got a big mouth sometimes...but he's a stand-up guy...Too good for the lousy scum out in Hollywood" (Giancana and Giancana 1992: 361).

In 1960 Sinatra introduced Giancana's lover Judith Campbell to John F. Kennedy and the two commenced a damaging affair. Giancana encouraged the relationship, as he did with Kennedy's tendency toward promiscuity in general. His strategy was to build up a file of incriminating information that could be used against the President and advance Mafia interests if circumstances required. Edgar J. Hoover, the director of the FBI, was also aware of Kennedy's relationship with Campbell. However, he concealed the information using the same logic as Giancana, namely that it could be a useful lever to advance FBI interests if needs be in the future. In the event, the assassination of Kennedy on November 22, 1963 prevented the information from being made public until the 1970s.

At the behest of the Kennedy's, Sinatra is alleged to have persuaded Giancana to use his influence over labor unions to engage in vote-rigging in the politically crucial West Virginia primary elections during the 1960 Kennedy presidential campaign. Giancana was rumored to have assembled a $50,000 war chest, using money from the Teamsters Central States Pension Fund, and to have delegated Skinny D'Amato to bribe state officials. Kennedy defeated Hubert Humphrey 60 to 40. The win was crucial in Kennedy's campaign for presidential office. It forced Humphrey to withdraw from the race and left Kennedy as the Democratic frontrunner.

Of course, Giancana was not motivated by any deep belief in Kennedy's political platform. From his standpoint, he successfully delivered the standard Mafia practice of producing a "favor" on the tacit assumption of unparticularized reciprocity from the new President in the future. In essence, he sought latitude from the Kennedys with respect to the FBI campaign against organized crime. In the event he was bitterly disappointed. As Attorney General, Robert Kennedy made the attack against organized crime the central plank of his period of office. Giancana became enraged with the Kennedys, and blamed Sinatra for leading him to a poisoned well. Under Mafia pressure, Sinatra attempted to backtrack with Robert Kennedy, but to no avail. An FBI transcript of a bugged conversation between Giancana and one of his associates, Johnny Formosa or Johnny Roselli, states:

> Johnny: I said "Frankie, can I ask one question?" He says, "Johnny, I took Sam's name and wrote it down and told Bobby Kennedy, 'This is my buddy. This is my buddy. This is what I want you to know, Bob'"...Between you and I, Frankie saw Joe Kennedy three different times. He called him three times, Joe Kennedy, the father.
> Giancana: He better make it, because after this administration goes out, he'll have a headache.
> Johnny: He says "Johnny, I have to protect myself."
> Giancana: He'll protect himself.
> Johnny: I say he [JFK] is a one-termer. He [Sinatra] says, "I got to watch myself." He says he's got an idea that you're mad at him. I says that I wouldn't know.
> Giancana: He must have a guilty conscience. I never said nothing...If he [JFK] starts campaigning, I'm not giving him one

penny... That (expletive) better not think of taking that (expletive) state... after all, if I'm taking somebody's money, I'm gonna make sure that this money is going to do something. Like, "Do you want it or don't you want it?" If the money is accepted, maybe one of these days, the guy will do me a favor.

Johnny: That's right. He [Sinatra] says he wrote your name down.

Giancana: Well, one minute he tells me this and then he tells me that. And then the last time I talked to him was at the hotel in Florida, a month before he left, and he said, "Don't worry about it, if I can't talk to the old man [Joe Kennedy], I'm going to talk to *the* man [JFK]." One minute he says he talked to Robert, and the next minute he says he hasn't talked to him. So he never did talk to him. It's a lot of (expletive). Either he did or he didn't. Forget about it. Why lie to me? I haven't got that coming.

Johnny: I can imagine... Tsk, tsk, tsk... if he can't deliver, I want him to tell me: "John, the load's too heavy."

Giancana: That's all right. At least you know how to work. You don't let your guard down then, know what I mean... Ask him [Sinatra] if I'm going to be invited to his New Year's party.

Johnny: I told him that's where I usually go for New Year's with Sam. But he says, "I have to be in Rome the twenty seventh."

Giancana: Too (expletive) bad. Tell him the Kennedys will keep him company.

Johnny: Why don't you talk to him [Sinatra]?

Giancana: When he says he's gonna do a guy a little favor, I don't give an (expletive) how long it takes. He's got to give you a little favor.

On December 21, 1961, Roselli and Giancana return to the subject of Sinatra and the Kennedys. The FBI transcript reads:

Johnny: He's got big ideas, Frank does, about being an ambassador or something. You know, Pierre Salinger [advisor to John Kennedy] and them guys, they don't want him. They treat him like they treat a whore. You (expletive) them, you pay them, and then they're through. You got the right idea, Moe [Giancana] – go the other way: (expletive) everybody. Every (expletive), we'll use them every (expletive) way we can. They only know one way. Now let them see the other side of you.

On January 4, 1962, Giancana returns to the same theme with an unidentified associate:

Giancana: Got a new law here where we can't go back and forth to the courts. Bobby Kennedy's bright idea.

Associate: How about his friend, and your friend, Sinatra?

Giancana: Aw, that (expletive). Johnny Roselli is out there. I told John to tell him to forget about the whole thing and tell him to go (expletive). Lying (expletive). If I ever listen to that (expletive) again – if he [JFK] had lost this state here, he would have lost the election. But I figured with this guy [Sinatra], maybe we'll be all right. I might have known this guy would (expletive) me.

Associate: Well, at the same time, it looks like you've done the right thing Sam. Nobody can say different, after it's done.

Giancana: Well, when a (expletive) lies to you ...

Associate: What was his motive?

Giancana: Who knows?

And again, on September 13, 1962:

Giancana: That Frank, he wants more money, he wants this, he wants that, he wants more girls, he wants ... I don't need that or him ... I broke my (expletive) when I was talking to him in New York.

Sinatra's inability to persuade the Kennedys to adopt a relaxed policy on organized crime precipitated demands for revenge. An FBI wiretap of a conversation between Giancana and an associate, Johnny Formosa, recorded the following interchange:

Formosa: Let's show 'em. Let's show those asshole Hollywood fruitcakes that they can't get away with it as if nothing's happened. Let's hit Sinatra. Or I could whack out a couple of those other guys [Peter] Lawford and that [Dean] Martin, and I could take out the nigger [Sammy Davis Jr] and put his other eye out.

Giancana: No ... I've got other plans for them.

The centerpiece of these other plans was to arrange for Sinatra, Dean Martin, Sammy Davis Jr and Eddie Fisher to open Giancana's new nightclub, the Villa Venice, in 1962. They duly did so in November of 1962, performing 16 shows in seven nights. None of the performers received a fee, prompting Dean Martin to improvise the following lyrics on stage to the tune of *The Lady Is a Tramp*:

> I love Chicago, it's carefree and gay
> I'd even work here, without any pay
> I'll lay you odds it turns out that way
> That's why this gentleman is a tramp.

Giancana was too much of a businessman to be affronted by Rat Pack sarcasm. His relationship with Sinatra persisted. In fact it was Giancana who inadvertently deprived Sinatra of his Nevada gambling license. Despite being listed in the Nevada Gaming Control Board's "Black Book" as a person debarred from having access to the gambling facilities in Nevada, Giancana stayed at Sinatra's Cal-Neva Lodge, Lake Tahoe, on two separate occasions in July 1963. As I noted in chapter 1, the public humiliation of being forced to sell Cal-Neva and his financial interests in the Sands Casino rankled with Sinatra for nigh on two decades, and was a significant factor in his drift toward the right in the late 1960s.

Further suggestions about Sinatra's involvement with Giancana emerged from the murky circumstances surrounding Marilyn Monroe's death. Munn (2001), who interviewed Ava Gardner at length, alleges that Sinatra withheld evidence on the death of Monroe. Munn submits that she did not commit suicide. She was murdered by a team of assassins organized by Johnny Roselli at the behest of Sam Giancana. Sinatra had introduced Monroe to John F. Kennedy and was aware of the affair between them. Monroe also had sexual relations with Robert Kennedy. Spurned by both of them, and under the influence of alcohol and drug dependence, she is alleged to have confessed to Giancana during a stay at the Cal-Neva Lodge that she intended to go public about her sexual relations with the Kennedys. According to Munn, Giancana regarded this as breaking the Mafia code of *omerta*, and more pressingly, undermining his power of intimidation over the President. Murdering Monroe would create the possibility of implicating Robert Kennedy, who, as Attorney General, was bearing down hard on Mafia operations. Giancana saw the possibility, at one stroke, of destroying Robert Kennedy and increasing his influence over John F. Kennedy. After Monroe's death from an apparent barbiturate overdose, Sinatra uncovered the plot, but withheld evidence from the police after receiving threats from Giancana.

Munn's is a byzantine theory that relies on Ava Gardner's verbal testimony. To date no solid independent evidence has emerged to corroborate his account. This is not to say that it is false. The psychology of power brokering, the blatant attempt to intimidate and generate favors, and the dispassionate attitude to murder are all known traits of Mafia behavior, and even in 1963 Giancana was an infamous pastmaster in this code of practice. However, pending independent corroborative evidence, Munn's account must rest as an interesting hypothesis rather than incontrovertible further proof of Sinatra's involvement with the Mafia.

In 1963 another incident occurred which has led to speculation that Sinatra was implicated in a Mob murder. A married worker at the Cal-Neva Lodge, Toni Morrison, had an affair with Sinatra which she eventually disclosed to her husband, deputy sheriff Richard Anderson. Anderson arrived at the Cal-Neva to confront Sinatra and in the ensuing altercation Sinatra was injured and unable to perform for several days (Freedland 1997: 306; Quirk and Schoell 1998: 147). One week later, Anderson and his wife were driving along a cliff road when his car was rammed and smashed into a tree. Anderson was killed, but his wife survived. No evidence supports the proposition that Sinatra directly arranged the crash. However, he is suspected of raising the "problem" of Anderson with his Mafia associates and it is speculated that Giancana used the incident to blackmail him. According to Munn:

Sinatra had spoken to his Cal-Neva partner Skinny D'Amato and said that he wanted the deputy sheriff to have "a little scare." D'Amato was believed by the FBI to be one of Giancana's "enforcers," and as such he was at Frank's disposal. So D'Amato arranged for the incident...What Frank didn't know then – although he found out later – was that D'Amato had had words with Giancana about it, and Giancana had said, "Just kill the fucking guy." (2001: 135–6)

Although this rationale is speculative, it is consistent with what is known about Giancana's modus operandi. Murdering Anderson provided Sinatra with a favor, but also acted as the basis for reciprocity in the future. Implicating Sinatra in a murder rather than a "scare" further weakened Sinatra's capacity for autonomy. It rendered him more beholden to Giancana for fear of being exposed as the putative sponsor of the crash. No solid evidence exists to confirm the involvement of D'Amato and Giancana in the accident. On the other hand, the vehicle that forced Anderson's car over the cliff was never traced and the incident remains unsolved.

FBI files indicate that Sinatra maintained contact with Giancana after the revocation of his gambling license. A memorandum dated August 21, 1967 to White House aide Mrs Mildred Stegall advised: "Our files reveal that Frank Sinatra continues to associate both socially and on a business basis with alleged members of La Cosa Nostra and other members of the hoodlum element in this country. Notable among such associates are Sam Giancana, Chicago, Illinois ... and Joseph Fischetti, Miami, Florida." As this memorandum extract implies, FBI investigations allege business connections between Sinatra and known Mafia-controlled interests. In 1954 he bought a 2 percent stake in the Mafia-controlled Sands Hotel, Las Vegas. This eventually rose to 9 percent. Among the perks he received was free, no-limit gambling in the casino. FBI files list the following Mafia personnel as being implicated with the hotel:

• Joseph "Doc" Stacher, who ran the hotel and had close links with Meyer Lansky. Stacher's police record included arrests for assault and battery, larceny, murder, bootlegging, hijacking, and murder.

- Charles "Babe" Baron, the official "greeter" at the hotel, with a record of suspected murder.
- Joe Fusco, a former member of Al Capone's gang.
- Meyer Lansky, as a Jew the highest-ranking non-Italian in the American Mafia. Lansky was the partner of Lucky Luciano and provided financial and physical muscle to support Bugsy Siegel's plan of investing in Las Vegas as the entertainment capital of the US.
- Abner "Longy" Zwillman, an associate of Willie Moretti and Meyer Lansky.
- Anthony "Tony Batters" Accardo, former bodyguard of Al Capone.
- Johnny Roselli, Giancana's representative in Las Vegas. He was involved in the FBI-sponsored plot to assassinate Castro in the early 1960s.

From the early 1950s until Howard Hughes acquired ownership in 1967, Sinatra appeared regularly at the Mafia-owned Desert Inn in Las Vegas. Sam Giancana and Meyer Lansky were suspected of having major financial interests in the hotel. Sinatra was partly attracted by the availability of free money. He was alleged to scam funds from Caesar's Palace by cashing in chips he had received gratis. In 1970 Sinatra was involved in an altercation with Sanford Waterman, a convicted racketeer and manager of the Palace. Waterman accused Sinatra of fleecing the casino of money. Sinatra responded violently and Waterman drew a pistol on him. Sinatra pressed assault charges against Waterman but was forced to drop them because there were visible marks on Waterman's throat (where Sinatra had tried to throttle him).

Sinatra was involved in the ownership of the Berkshire Downs Racetrack in Western Massachusetts. The FBI suspected that he was a front for Raymond Patriarca and Gaetano "Three-Fingers Brown" Lucchese. Patriarca was the head of the Mafia in Providence, Rhode Island and by the mid-1950s his organization had spread throughout New England. In 1972 the Senate's Select

Committee on Crime prepared a subpoena for Sinatra to question him about his involvement in the ownership of the racetrack. The intervention of Senator John Tunney of California prevented the subpoena from being issued. Tunney assured the Committee that Sinatra was prepared to voluntarily cooperate with investigations. The Committee invited Sinatra to appear before them on June 4, 1972. Instead Sinatra fled to the UK. The Committee prepared a second subpoena and ordered US marshals to serve it as soon as Sinatra set foot again on US soil. Sinatra enlisted the assistance of Vice President Spiro T. Agnew to have the subpoena rescinded. He appeared before the Committee on July 18 and denied any connection with the Mafia. Raymond Patriarca was brought before the Committee from the Atlanta Federal Penitentiary where he was serving a ten-year sentence for conspiracy to murder. His testimony was a triumph of evasion and double-think. Asked if he knew Sinatra, Patriarca replied:

> A: I never met Sinatra personally. I seen him on television and at the moving pictures.
> Q: Did you ever have any business dealings with him?
> A: No, sir.
> Q: Did you ever purchase stock from him?
> A: No, sir.
> Q: Anybody on your behalf do it?
> A: I claim my Fifth Amendment privilege.
> Q: Do you have any knowledge that anyone associated with you had any business dealings with Sinatra?
> A: I claim my Fifth Amendment privilege.

Sinatra was never charged. But he was embarrassed by this highly public inquisition into his private life. He adopted the standard Mafia practice of protesting innocence and maintaining *omerta*, the code of silence, with respect to his own illegal conduct and the illegal conduct of any known Mafia associates. He also complained of harassment by the authorities. For example, he was petulant with the Committee, sending them a bill for $18,750 in expenses, which was never paid. Similarly, in an article in the *New York Times* he complained that the Committee had invaded his privacy in order to make political capital in an election year. The Committee withdrew and no further action was taken in the Berkshire Downs case.

FBI files also imply that Sinatra intervened to secure the pardon of a convicted Mafia executioner, Angelo "Gyp" DeCarlo. A brief dated May 24, 1973 reports:

A source who has furnished reliable information in the past advised on January 3, 1973, that Frank Sinatra is a close friend of Angelo DeCarlo of long standing. Sources who have furnished reliable information in the past have described DeCarlo as a respected member of organized crime in the United States who holds a position of *caporegima* in the Genovese family of La Cosa Nostra.

On December 21, 1972 DeCarlo was released from United States penitentiary, Lewisberg, Pennsylvania, after a commutation of his sentence by Presidential order. A source who has furnished reliable information in the past advised that DeCarlo's release came as no real surprise to certain associates of DeCarlo as they had been informed by someone very close to DeCarlo that he was expected to be released before Christmas.

This source further stated that these same associates are attributing DeCarlo's release to the intervention of singer Frank Sinatra, whose close personal relationship with Vice President Spiro Agnew allegedly served as the necessary "contact." The source stated that Sinatra's efforts had allegedly been in the works for "at least a couple of months."

Information concerning Sinatra's friendship with DeCarlo and DeCarlo's release from Federal custody was furnished to the Department by Newark's letterhead memorandum dated January 11, 1973 ... Frank Sinatra allegedly turned over $100,000 cash to Maurice Sterns as an unrecorded contribution (to Nixon's re-election campaign fund). Subsequently, due to the fact that Vice President Agnew had been "stripped of his authority by White House aides," one Peter Maletasta allegedly contacted former Presidential Counsel John Dean and got him to make the necessary arrangements to forward the request to the Justice Department. Sinatra then allegedly "made a $50,000 contribution to the President's campaign fund sometime during December 1972. DeCarlo's release followed."

93

One should note that DeCarlo was imprisoned in 1970 for conspiracy to commit murder. He was pardoned, ostensibly on the grounds that he was terminally ill. In fact DeCarlo died a year later of cancer, but upon his release he was rumored to boast about Sinatra's influence to win favors with the American power elite. FBI investigations ultimately ruled that there was no proof that Sinatra had connived with Nixon and Agnew to secure DeCarlo's release. However, the Chair of the Senate Permanent Committee on Investigations eventually ruled that the pardon "bypassed normal procedures and safeguards." The investigation invited serious charges against President Nixon, the US Marshal Service, and the IRS. However, further investigation was preempted by Agnew's resignation and the Watergate scandal. No formal charges were ever made against Sinatra.

Sinatra is also known to have associated with Carlo Gambino, head of the premier crime family in New York. Gambino was implicated in the murder of Albert "The Executioner" Anastasia. The assassination promoted Vito Genovese and Gambino to head their respective Mafia families in 1957. Upon Genovese's death in 1967, Gambino became the effective *capo di tutti capi* of the American Mafia.

Sinatra was involved in two business deals with him. In 1970 both invested in a company called Computer Fields Expressway, and in 1974 they invested in the Westchester Premier Theatre in Tarrytown, New York. The Westchester was the scene of the infamous photograph showing Sinatra backstage and arm in arm with Gambino and his praetorian guard. Pictured with Gambino and Sinatra are Gregory De Palma, Aladena "Jimmy the Weasel" Fratiano, Joseph Gambino Jr, and Paul Castellano. These were notorious figures in the East Coast Mafia:

- Gregory De Palma was a mob lieutenant, eventually sentenced to six years for labor racketeering, tax crimes, and extortion.
- Fratianno was associated with the Los Angeles crime family under the leadership of Jack Dragna. He was implicated in the murder of mob rivals Tony Bracato and Anthony Trombino.

- Paul Castellano was a convicted robber, married to Carlo Gambino's sister-in-law, and implicated in the murders of his son-in-law Frank Amato and Roy de Meo. He was selected by Carlo Gambino over Aneillo "Mr Neil" Dellacore, mentor of John Gotti, to head the family after Gambino's death in 1976, but is generally thought to have been a weak and vacillating leader. He was murdered by John Gotti's hitmen in 1985. Gotti went on to become the new boss of the Gambino family.

In sum, the material relating to Sinatra's Mafia connections in the FBI files presents a compelling case that Sinatra had long-standing social connections with leading Mafia figures, participated in business deals with some of them, and performed for them on request. He appears to have been especially close to Sam Giancana, head of the Chicago syndicate. When confronted by his daughter Tina in the early 1990s about the fact that Giancana was a known murderer, Sinatra replied, "I never reacted beyond how he treated me. I wasn't unaware of what he was, and I didn't bring him to your First Communion, but he was always decent to me" (T. Sinatra 2000: 74). Jimmy Roselli's taunt that Sinatra would have willingly given up his singing career to be a don may have been hyperbole. Nonetheless, the evidence suggests that Sinatra valued his friendship with mob bosses highly. He admired the direct and morally unencumbered route that the Mafia took to the acquisition of power. On several occasions the connections put his career at risk when he was petitioned by state and federal committees of investigation to explain his suspected links with Mafia personnel and business interests. Power by association is one thing, but in the case of the death of Sheriff Anderson, and the part ownership of the Sands and Cal-Neva casinos, the Berkshire Downs Racetrack, the Westchester Premier Theater and the Computer Fields Expressway the evidence points to collaborative business relationships. Sinatra's Caesarism, his audacity, immorality, self-righteousness and deep-seated menace found sympathetic parallels in the figure of the mafioso.

three

ANTINOMIES OF ACHIEVED CELEBRITY

Sinatra's capacity for self-discipline was quixotic. He could be careless, imperious and inscrutable, but if a project took his fancy, or if he wished to create a good impression, he could be punctilious to an excruciating degree. For example, he involved himself in all aspects of his famous Columbia and Capitol recording sessions in the 1940s and 1950s, taking pains to ensure that he had eye contact with all of the orchestra, and not hesitating to challenge the arranger if he was dissatisfied with the sound. He acquired the reputation of being a military martinet in the recording studio at this time. The pianist Stan Freedman comments: "I remember him being very aware of what he wanted, and getting it! If he thought a lute or oboe part should be left out of one section, he would say so. He didn't have to take charge, but nominally he was in charge – and everybody knew that" (quoted in Granata 1999: 56). Similarly, the Rat Pack shows of the late 1950s and early 1960s, which audiences took to be ramshackle, unscripted and performed in an alcoholic haze, were actually carefully choreographed and generally soberly presented.

The military simile is appropriate. Sinatra never served in the armed forces, but his attitude and demeanor were often soldierly, especially in his later years. The sententious bravado of *My Way*, the highly public barracking and commandeering of the Rat Pack, his obsessive preoccupation with the correct form of public dress, his barbed-wire patriotism, his sensitivity to hidden "enemies" and "threats," his respect for manly endurance, especially as exhibited in his astonishing consumption of alcohol (by his early forties he was said to drink one bottle of Jack Daniels whisky a day, to say nothing of the two dry martinis he favored before dinner and the French and Italian reds, notably Petrus, Mouton Rothschild, Gaja and Margaux, in the evening), his gruelling performance work-rate (between 1960 and 1965 he gave 200 nightclub performances per year which were organized around a prolific film and recording output (T. Sinatra 2000: 101)), and his habit of portraying himself as "the leader" or the "chairman of the board" – all smacked of old-fashioned soldierly traits.

For most celebrities, as for most of the public during the war years, patriotism was an issue that overrode party political considerations. The general American worldview then, as now, presupposed the preeminence of the American way. Consequently the war in Europe and Japan was regarded not merely as an attack on fascism but also an opportunity to prove the superior worth of Americanism throughout the world. This outlook is understandable, but it was based on negligible and inadequate appreciation of economic, political and cultural conditions in ethnic America, let alone circumstances in other countries.

In fact Sinatra was unusual among white performers in having a good deal of firsthand knowledge about the conditions of black ethnic minorities in the US. From the late 1930s he mixed with black jazz musicians in New York, Los Angeles, and Chicago. In many ways the racism they suffered was congruent with his experience as an Italian-American in ethnically divided Hoboken. He certainly recognized affinities and in the 1950s and 1960s he was closely associated with the civil rights movement.

Yet for all his left-leaning public statements in the 1940s and early 1950s, he prominently supported the American way and shared media and popular anxieties about the so-called "Communist Menace." In 1948, together with Italian-American celebrities Jimmy Durante and Joe Di Maggio, and Hollywood stars Gary Cooper and Bing Crosby, Sinatra made radio propaganda broadcasts to Italy during the elections, warning electors of the menace of Communism. The broadcasts were officially volunteer activities underwritten by prominent Italian-American Catholics, such as Archbishop Cardinal Spellman of New York. They were part of a wider US government campaign to deliver the elections in Italy out of the hands of the left. Christopher Simpson (1988: 90–1) identifies this as the first major covert operations and propaganda effort of the then newly founded CIA. It involved multimillion dollar operations ranging from the clandestine sponsorship of anti-Communist articles in influential newspapers to bankrolling thugs to beat up and harass prominent Communist candidates and their sympathizers.

There is no proof that Sinatra knew of CIA sponsorship in either the radio broadcasts to Italy or the "dirty tricks" campaign. On the other hand, Sinatra was worldly enough to appreciate the political significance of the broadcasts. Sinatra's public actions against the far left did not end with this episode. Although he was a sincere and courageous opponent of McCarthyism, he shared many aspects of the Cold War mentality. In 1951 he participated in an anti-Communist rally in Central Park sponsored by the Stop Communism Committee (Meyer 2002: 325–6). By the mid-1950s, when faced with the choice of reaffirming his youthful leftism or identifying with American imperial interests in Korea and later Vietnam and Iran, Sinatra consistently favored the latter option. He remained an American patriot, but by the 1970s cared little if his patriotism was nailed to a Democrat or a Republican mast. The quest for power and influence overrode political considerations.

Hollywood made enormous capital out of the patriotic frenzy of the war years and the aftermath of victory. The struggle against the Nazi Axis powers and Japan was glorified in countless film plots and sequels. Ironically, during the war Hollywood was notably reluctant to encourage its entourage of eligible male celebrities to enlist. Gene Autry, who joined the Army, Henry Fonda and Robert Montgomery, who served in the Navy, Tyrone Power, who served in the Marines, Clark Gable, who enlisted in the Army Air Corps and worked for Army Intelligence, and James Stewart, who gained many decorations in the Air Force, were exceptions to the rule. Most followed the path of Sinatra and the great *faux* war hero John Wayne, and devoted themselves to careerist maneuvering at home.[1]

Sinatra at War

Sinatra's war was fought on film lots in California. Inasmuch as this is so, he had a good war. He played the role of a member of the Armed Forces in 12 of his 44 movies. He was a decorated sailor in the American Navy in *Anchors Away* (1945) and a nondecorated naval rating in *On the Town* (1949); a victimized Army private in *From Here to Eternity* (1953); a former World War Two infantryman turned would-be assassin of the President in *Suddenly* (1954); an Army lieutenant in *Kings Go Forth* (1958); a bitter demobbed Army writer in *Some Came Running* (1958); a captain in the Overseas Special Services unit in *Never So Few* (1959); a corrupt former commando and gang leader in the first Rat Pack film, *Ocean's Eleven* (1960); a brainwashed military hero in *The Manchurian Candidate* (1962); a prisoner of war of the Japanese in *None But the Brave* (1965), which Sinatra also directed; a prisoner of war and escapee from the Germans and Italians in *Von Ryan's Express* (1965); a submarine lieutenant in *Assault on a Queen* (1966); and a former Army sniper in *The Naked Runner* (1967). He never became a symbol of the warrior class or a military hero in the manner of John Wayne. Famously, on a visit to Japan in 1975, Wayne was embarrassed to be greeted by Emperor Hirohito with the remark that he "must have killed off the entire Japanese army" (Roberts and Olson 1995: 3). Sinatra's public reputation as a devotee of the high life and a performer who was known to associate with Mafia leaders and henchmen ensured that similar claims would never be made on his behalf. However, like Wayne, Sinatra identified strongly with the symbolism and gravitas of military bearing. He approved of the assurance, moral gravity and authority that the role of the warrior conveyed. In his public life, when it suited, he did not stint at playing the part despite occupying it by proxy.

Ironically, the young Sinatra was at first held in bad odor by the majority of troops in the 1940s. He began his postwar tours with the United Services Organization (USO) as a deeply unpopular figure. He was generally perceived to be a spoiled malingerer who was suspected of deploying special connections to avoid the draft. In addition, he was regarded as having spent the war years surrounded by an adoring, predominantly female audience, patiently amassing a vast personal fortune. But Sinatra swiftly won over critics by playing the self-effacing straight man to the acerbic popular comedian Phil Silvers on stage, and by his obvious concern for the wounded soldiers he met in hospital camps. Sinatra was never an unmitigated cynical celebrity. He always remembered both his unprepossessing background in Hoboken and the fact that other people of his generation had been left behind while he was elevated in the public eye. He often found it hard to identify with these people and the stories of his indifference and harsh rejection of fans are as legion as testaments of his generosity.

Perhaps of fundamental importance is Sinatra's sense of himself and his immediate circle as parvenus. Although Sinatra was an abrupt, authoritarian personality in many respects, infamous for riding roughshod over the opinions of others to pursue his own desires and whims, he was overtly antiauthoritarian in his attitude to power elites and officialdom. In most of his military roles he usually identified with the rank-and-file serviceman or the promoted enlisted man, seldom the commanding officer. Maggio, in *From Here to Eternity*, was the archetype; but John Baron, the discharged infantryman turned would-be assassin of the President in *Suddenly*, David Hirsh, the embittered poet-warrior in *Some Came Running*, the former blue-collar worker, Lieutenant Loggins, in *Kings Go Forth*, and semi-brainwashed Major Bennett Marco in *The Manchurian Candidate* followed suit. John Baron has some lines in *Suddenly* that arguably epitomize Sinatra's view of contributions and rank in war time: "I killed more Gerries than any five officers put together. I did some pretty good chopping in the war. Pretty good...My CO used to stand there shaking like a leaf while I chopped."

Sinatra returned from his overseas tour of troops organized by the USO to disparage the top brass as "shoemakers in uniform."

The comment attracted the attention of his old enemy, the Hearst newspaper columnist Lee Mortimer, who employed it to question the sincerity of his patriotism. It is generally considered to have soured the goodwill that his overseas tour amassed (Clarke 1997: 101; Taraborrelli 1997: 107).

Nonetheless, a popular view of Sinatra as a surrogate old soldier took root later in his career, especially when his declining health became unmistakable. In later life Sinatra was the recipient of the Presidential Medal of Freedom and the Congressional Gold Medal. But these were civil honors that carried no military status or rights. When he died, President Clinton took the most unusual step of authorizing a full military funeral. Sinatra's widow, Barbara Marx, and her lawyer opposed the gesture on grounds of taste, much to the dismay of Sinatra's children. In the event a compromise was struck and Sinatra was laid to rest in Palm Springs with a reduced military guard of honor. At the end of the ceremony a marine presented the American flag to Barbara "on behalf of a grateful nation" (T. Sinatra 2000: 299).

But for what was the American nation being grateful? President Clinton, in his unctuous written eulogy on Sinatra, refers to his "miraculous," "spellbinding" performing skills and says he dedicated himself to humanitarian causes.[2] But in reality, Sinatra presents an ambivalent model of achieved celebrity to the world. He could be gallant, loyal, magnanimous, decisive, courageous, and generous. But throughout his public career a darker, disturbing side to his personality was palpable, one which savored adventurism, amorality, violence, intimidation and bribery to achieve ends. Informed critical opinion identified him as a consort of Mafia bosses, a four times married male who spent a large part of his life as a serial adulterer, a notoriously heavy drinker, a reckless gambler, a spiteful adversary capable of dwelling for decades on revenge, and a bully well versed in the practices of intimidation and menace. His material success, charitable works and the obvious affection in which he held his children and grandchildren were mired by the pubic perception of him as, in David Thomson's words, "foul-mouthed, bad tempered and so vicious that he often beat people up" (2002: 1).

The Psychology of Achieved Celebrity

Sinatra was an achieved celebrity, arguably one of the most resplendent in the field of American popular entertainment in the twentieth century. This popularity derived in part from his relatively humble beginnings. Yet he was both insufferably proud of and tormented by his parvenu status. This left an indelible mark on his psychology as an achieved celebrity. Until the end of his days he made no bones about emerging from the ranks of the people. Yet at the same time he was fully aware that the scale of his success estranged him from them. This sense of the loss of his roots was not replaced by corresponding feelings of belonging to the higher echelons of the wealthy of which his material success now made him a part. As a member of the Hollywood celebritariat he was regarded as a rough diamond by old money. This reinforced his desire for legitimacy and this was expressed in his obsession with power.

Sinatra learned that financial achievement and celebrity status are not sufficient to open all doors in American life. His relations with the establishment bear the watermark of not being acknowledged as "one of us," a lack of acceptance that was a continuous thorn in Sinatra's side. Arguably, it is the American dilemma, especially of first born citizens, who more than the native born suffer from a sense of displacement and estrangement: achievement without acceptance. After all, why had Sinatra's parents left Italy? To find a new life or to escape the shame of being rejected by the homeland? The sense of what might be called, perhaps portentously, *primordial* rejection never left Sinatra. However good he was as an entertainer, businessman or political fixer, however rich he became, he could never overcome the sense of belonging to cast-off stock. The anxiety of being profoundly, unutterably *dispossessed* arguably haunts the psyche of migrants into the American melting pot. If so, Sinatra dealt with it by developing a relationship to politics and public respectability that was at once passionate and lethally tenuous.

Notoriously, in his middle and later years he switched from youthful evangelicalism for the Democrats to dyed-in-the-wool support for the Republicans. In truth his attitude to power was promiscuous and ultimately self-serving. He was attracted to power as an end in itself, for the bearing it gave the holder in public. Leaving aside the desire to perfect his vocal art, one of the few consistencies in Sinatra's career was the determination to be recognized as a person of cultural and physical substance, a man able to fix problems swiftly and decisively, a man indeed who craved acceptance. As noted in chapter 2, to some degree this reflects the Sicilian male ideal, which fulfills its most extreme expression in the figure of the mafioso. But it also reveals the flexibility of an achieved celebrity of Sinatra's stature, who is positioned to move relatively freely between the interlocking circles of economic, political and military influence, and whose fame yields a measure of immunity from prosecution.

Achieved celebrities frequently complain that their psychology is uncomfortably displaced. They are not at home in themselves, and they feel themselves to be expatriates from their home background. While they often make extravagant public displays about the decency of ordinary folk and family values, most of them would no more dream of returning to live in their home neighborhoods than abandoning their celebrity status. Achieved celebrity is a different world. While sentimental expressions of the old days come easily to many achieved celebrities, they maintain great care to protect their wealth, lifestyle, and celebrity status. It is given to relatively few people to walk into a room and be immediately recognized as the unequivocal centre of attention. Still fewer receive the economic riches that are the due of the highest echelon of achieved celebrity. The honor and wealth distributed to achieved celebrities are intoxicating. They literally give the recipient a drunken sense of his or her self-importance.

Conversely, they also involve excessive intrusion, leaving the celebrity with a sense of being harassed by the public or dogged by counterfeit relations with others. Achieved celebrities frequently testify to the emptiness of the honorific rituals of celebrity status and materialism. They compare achieved success to a no man's land in which they are neither fish nor fowl. Chris Evans, the British disc jockey, show business tycoon and game show host, is reported to have said that when you get to the top you find there is nothing there (Gray 2002: 7). This point of view abounds in the literature of celebrity with such profusion that it has become a cliché. Even so, it remains an indispensable insight into the psychology of achieved celebrity.

Sociologists use the term *anomie* to describe a condition in which there is a lack of certainty about values and goals, and an absence of a binding moral, normative framework to guide choice and action. Achieved celebrity is inherently *anomic* since it plucks the individual from the ground rules of domestic life and elevates him or her into a world in which the boundaries of conduct are infinitely more elastic. One coping strategy is to offer exaggerated panegyrics to one's roots from the dizzy heights of one's achievement. The abandoned home becomes the imaginary moral anchor for relations in the new and uncertain world of glamour, power, prestige, and wealth. Celebrities often invoke the moral certainties of home against the glittering, meretricious world of fame, conveniently forgetting the determination that they generally harnessed to escape the trappings of their family and neighborhood of origin, and overlooking the tenacity with which they strive to hold on to their achieved status.

In Sinatra's case, he offered countless tributes to the values of his family and the Italian-American community of his youth. He credited them with instilling in him beliefs in fair play, racial tolerance, and giving a break to the little man. He was less supportive of Hoboken, a town that he rarely visited after achieving his success and which he regarded as having held him in insufficient esteem. In public declarations he offered the traditional gospel of self-help as his philosophy of making good. For example, in the 1970s he went on record with a German interviewer as maintaining: "You've got to put the most into everything that you do. You must try to do the best, with a decency and a dignity and compassion for your fellow man. I think that if you do the best you can in your life, you get your just reward." (quoted in Zehme 1997: 246)

Sinatra believed in concepts of "dignity" and "compassion," but he did so on his own terms. His moral code was paleolithic.

In his business and personal relationships he punished infraction and transgression with violence, occasionally with physical attacks and usually with implacable social and psychological rejection. He held a black-and-white view of friendship and love, demanding total loyalty but keeping his corresponding options open.

For example, onstage in 1966, during a performance at the Sands Hotel, he said of his third wife, Mia Farrow, 30 years younger than he was: "Maybe you wondered why I finally married her. Well, I finally found a broad I can cheat on" (cited in Freedland 1997: 233–4). This is a callous and mean-spirited remark which caused Farrow considerable public embarrassment. It is not only sexist, it relishes the age difference between the couple in a boorish, self-regarding way, relegating Farrow to a mere *naïf* and casting himself in the role of a world-weary, gin-marinated *savant*. He acts as if his glamour and fame insulate him from the ordinary duties of respectable marital behavior.

The achieved celebrity indeed passes from the ordinary world of habitual mutuality, reciprocity and respect into an altogether more imprecise world of inexhaustible possibility, global intrigue and fabulous wealth. Accountability to fans persists, but this is generally an abstract relationship managed by cultural intermediaries such as publicists, stylists and managers and punctuated by public performances designed to *elevate* the celebrity above the public rather than to engage in genuine mutuality and reciprocity. Achieved celebrities live on a different plane to the rest of us. Their sense of psychological integrity is undermined by public representations of their fame. For the public face is always an assisted, artificial construction, a design intended to have a cultural effect in stimulating desire and worship in the audience.

In presenting a public face, achieved celebrities often complain of symptoms of psychological disassociation. The public responds to a carefully constructed external face, but the real self is elsewhere and suffers from annihilating feelings of nonrecognition and, in some cases, invalidation. In the private life of celebrities accountability and loyalty are frangible and strategic.

105

This is why so many of them experience divorce, addictions to drugs and alcohol, and difficulties with siblings.

Sinatra himself divorced three times and had a somewhat thwarted relationship with his son, Frankie Junior. Junior was a more introspective, thoughtful character than his father. In choosing to be "his father *manqué*" by following a performing and recording career with the Tommy Dorsey Band, he opened himself up to the full range of Sinatra's invective, spite, and fatherly praise. Two weeks after the assassination of John F. Kennedy, Frankie Junior was the subject of a bizarre kidnap. He was held for some days and a ransom of $240,000 was paid. The kidnappers were eventually captured and most of the money was recovered.

In the final five years of his performing career Sinatra appointed Frankie Junior as his music conductor. But the public always regarded the relationship as uncomfortable. Sinatra seemed not so much to be assisting his son as adding a new layer in his overbearing attitude toward him. Perhaps his son made him competitive and overconscious of his own mortality. For an achieved celebrity of Sinatra's stature, physical disappearance – death – after having struggled so hard and with such accomplishment to attain achievement is an appalling prospect. This is why the charities and foundations they create cannot be read as simple acts of generosity. They are also investments in their enduring fame and cultural presence. This was certainly the case with Sinatra who feared death greatly and engaged liberally in charitable works in the last 25 years of his life.

Contra his troubled relationship with Frankie Junior, Sinatra was notably more affectionate and indulgent with his daughters, Nancy and Tina. Kitty Kelley (1986: 285) makes much of his favoritism to the girls, noting that they always received presents galore at Christmas, whereas Frankie Junior received scarcely $500 worth of gifts. Sinatra aided Nancy's singing career, duetting with her on the number one single *Somethin' Stupid*, a somewhat incestuous, ill-judged love song for a father and daughter to sing.

Sinatra and the End of Ageing

Between the ages of 38 and 70, that is, during the period between 1953 and 1985, there was a sense in which Sinatra decided to put the ageing process on hold. In these years he was a sort of middle-aged adolescent, concealing his baldness with hair transplants and toupees that cost $400 each (hair loss was the main reason why he adopted the trademark hat in the 1950s), carousing, flirting, holding fraternity house parties with his tribe, and showing wild, erratic mood swings. He had a perpetual concern with appearing to be up-to-date and cool. At one excruciating moment during his marriage to Mia Farrow he was photographed in love beads and a Nehru jacket. For much of this period he engaged in serial one-night stands and brief relationships, often with Las Vegas showgirls. One reason why he performed so regularly in Las Vegas during the 1950s and early 1960s was the resort's supply of available women. His contact with the Mafia, which is heavily active in the city, increased. His habit of throwing tantrums, dropping people without notice, and picking pointless fights was perhaps at its apogee.

Consider: in 1960 he met the actress and dancer Juliet Prowse on the set of the film *Can-Can*. Prowse was much younger than Sinatra and the relationship formed a prologue to his marriage with Mia Farrow. The affair lasted two years. Sinatra proposed, but after his troubled relationship with Ava Gardner, he was wary of marrying another performer whose career interest might compete with that of his own. He demanded that she abandon film and dancing. Prowse demurred, her caution reinforced by Sinatra's insistence that he was not interested in starting a second family. The relationship on offer was all on Sinatra's terms. Wealth, security and Hollywood status would be his part of the bargain. In return, the 45-year-old Sinatra expected to receive an attractive, intelligent, compliant partner who would manage his home life without cramping his freedom to party with his tribe of male friends and have the occasional discreet affair.

Throughout their two-year relationship, Prowse was aware that Sinatra saw other women. His affection was always conditional, and his worst actions were always legitimated by his reputation of being the greatest entertainer of the age. However, when she started seeing a dancer, Nick Nevara, in retaliation, Sinatra became incensed. As she put it: "He ... came to my apartment at three o'clock in the morning, banging on my door. And I wouldn't answer the door because I had Nick with me inside. He then disappeared screaming and yelling" (quoted in Freedland 1997: 281). Half an hour later she was called by Sinatra's secretary, Gloria Lovell, and advised that she should immediately vacate the building.

Sinatra didn't speak to Prowse for six months. When he called her again out of the blue he behaved as if nothing untoward had happened. He was magnanimous and solicitous. She was working in New York and, when she flew home, Sinatra insisted on meeting her at LAX (Los Angeles Airport). Whereupon he caused a sensation by meeting her alone, in his Italian Ghia, and with an engagement ring in his pocket. But the relationship slid into its familiar rut. Sinatra again demanded that she quit her career. He entered into relationships with other women, including Dorothy Provine, star of the TV series the *Roaring Twenties*. Prowse retaliated by commencing an affair with Elvis Presley. When Sinatra discovered this he again became furious and gave her an ultimatum. Again she demurred, and the relationship eventually petered out.

Sinatra often resorted to somewhat crass acts of emotional blackmail to get his way. In 1950 after an argument with Ava Gardner, he returned to his apartment in a huff. Early in the morning he phoned Gardner to inform her that he was about to commit suicide. He fired two shots and the phone went dead. Gardner rushed to his apartment only to find Sinatra bemused, indignant, but uninjured. He'd fired the bullets into his mattress. Although he regretted this incident later in life, it shows the shameless lengths to which he would go in order to manipulate the emotions of others, especially women.

In addition, his impulsive violence was always a threat, as much to friends as to foes. In the late 1950s he menaced Lucille

Ball's husband, the actor and film producer Desi Arnaz. Arnaz produced the popular TV series *The Untouchables*. Sinatra and the Mafia objected to it on the grounds that it gave Italians a bad name. It is typical of Sinatra to put himself forward as the spokesman for the Italian-American community without having solicited their opinion or mandate. Part of him acted like a radar on behalf of the imagined slights and indignities heaped upon others, especially the amorphous abstraction of "his people." He could be insufferably didactic about the problems of the little man, and electrically sensitive to perceived attacks on his own community. On a visit to the Indian Wells Country Club with his long-time friend, the songwriter Jimmy Van Heusen, he confronted Arnaz, only to be publicly rebuffed. Arnaz had taken the precaution of coming to the restaurant with body-guards. In a rage Sinatra returned to Van Heusen's apartment for a drink. On the wall was a Norman Rockwell portrait of Van Heusen. As the evening wore on, Sinatra's rage with Arnaz moved from intemperate to incandescent. Quirk and Schoell take up the story thus:

> [Suddenly] Sinatra took a knife to the irreplaceable, once-in-a-lifetime painting and slashed it to ribbons, pretending it was Arnaz, who had, in Frank's skewered view "humiliated" him. When Van Heusen began to scream in protest – "Frank! Why destroy my portrait?" – Frank bellowed at him, "You're bought and paid for Chester! Just shut-up or next time I'll take down the wall instead of a fucking painting." (1998: 145)[3]

Later Sinatra attempted to make reparation by sending Van Heusen an expensive Japanese print. But he badly misjudged the effect of his egregious behavior and ever after Van Heusen felt querulous about Sinatra's trustworthiness and capacity for self-control.

In his forties and fifties there are many other examples of Sinatra's impulsive violence which raise questions about his contact with reality. In the late 1950s, at a party at Gary Cooper's house, Sinatra attacked a young woman and pushed her through a plate glass window. Peter Lawford remembered:

It was horrifying. The worst I've ever seen Frank and I've seen him pretty bad. The girl's arm was nearly cut off! Judy Garland was at the party and I had to hold her up, she was fainting from the blood. For once I think the drugs and the liquor helped because it made everything seem so unreal. It was just a horror show. (Quoted in Quirk and Schoell 1998: 147)

The girl was hospitalized and paid to keep quiet.

Similarly, Munn (2001: 136–7) recounts a well-known story about Sinatra's assault on his valet of 20 years service, George Jacobs, during a flight on Sinatra's private aeroplane. Sinatra ordered Jacobs to fetch a hardboiled egg from the kitchen area. In error, Jacobs selected an uncooked egg. When Sinatra, who had a girl sitting on his lap, cracked it open he became demented. He pushed the girl from his lap and wrestled Jacobs to the door and flung it open. Dean Martin intervened and calmed the situation down. No one will ever know if Sinatra intended to throw Jacobs out of the plane. But the incident gives a revealing insight into his hairtrigger temper and code of rough justice.

In 1962 at Facks club in San Francisco a cameraman photographed him without his consent. A local San Francisco newspaper reported that Sinatra "leaped for the photographer's throat and wrestled him to the floor," and that club personnel "hustled Sinatra off to a cloakroom to allow him to cool off" (Shaw 1968: 304). For any celebrity, let alone a star of Sinatra's magnitude, it was rash, ill-judged behavior. But it was by no means an isolated incident.

In 1966 Sinatra was involved in an altercation at the Polo Lounge of the Beverly Hills Hotel which almost led to the death of a house guest. Sinatra was hosting a party for Dean Martin's forty-ninth birthday. Sitting at a nearby booth were Frederick R. Weisman, president of Hunt's Foods, and Franklin H. Fox, a businessman from Boston. Weisman complained that Sinatra's party was making too much noise. Randall Taraborrelli reports:

Frank was annoyed by Weisman's intrusion. "listen, buddy you're out of line," he warned Weisman. Angry words were exchanged and Frank got up and stormed out of the room.

A few moments later, he returned. He and Weisman then became embroiled in a verbal argument, and depending on which version of the story from which eyewitness is to be believed, Frank either decked the man by throwing a telephone at his head (the Polo Lounge had telephones in many of the booths), or the man just fell over the cocktail table and hit his head. Whatever the case, an unconscious Weisman was taken away by ambulance. (1997: 464–5)

Weisman's injury was serious, and potentially life-threatening. He suffered a fractured skull and remained in a coma for some time. The Los Angeles Police Department wanted to question Sinatra, but he had gone to ground. According to one friend, Sinatra was beside himself. "Now I've gone and done it," Sinatra said... "I've really fucked up. If this guy croaks, I'm fucking finished" (quoted in Taraborrelli 1997: 465). In the event Weisman recovered, and as he convalesced his family received anonymous, threatening phone calls which advised him not to press charges, with which he duly complied (Clarke 1997: 252).

How can this insolence toward women and impulsive violence against strangers be explained? Was Sinatra a pathological character? The evidence is weak. He was certainly vindictive, and nursed grudges that he showed no scruples in settling by recourse to physical assault if necessary. But aside from the circumstantial data implicating him in the murder of Sheriff Anderson, there is little tenable proof of a tendency toward premeditated assault. The grudges that he nursed were wrapped up in the fantasy world of being Frank Sinatra, the adored, invulnerable celebrity, anointed by his fans, who possessed the capacity to behave just as he pleased without a mind for the consequences.

The masculine ideal to which he subscribed legitimated the use of physical violence to achieve ends. Sinatra regularly returned to this theme in his film roles. The beleaguered Maggio resorts to physical violence against the bullying Sergeant "Fatso" Judson (played by Ernest Borgnine) in *From Here to Eternity*; Ryan reluctantly shoots the Italian female hostage in the back at a station near the border with Switzerland because she is about to alert the enemy that the train has been hijacked by Allied prisoners in *Von Ryan's Express*; and the businessman and former army sniper Sam Laker becomes righteously homicidal after being duped by British Intelligence in *The Naked Runner*. Vulnerability was a source of Sinatra's appeal in his early stage and recording career. It was prominent in some of his most successful film roles, such as the heroin addict Frankie Machine in *The Man with the Golden Arm* and Joe E. Lewis, the comedian and victim of gangland mutilation, in *The Joker Is Wild*. He also returned to explore it memorably in some of his classic Capitol albums in the 1950s, notably *In the Wee Small Hours*, *Where Are You?* and *Only the Lonely*.

But there is something stony and self-regarding about Sinatra's vulnerablity. His code of masculinity did not acknowledge personal frailty or vulnerability in men. The icy way in which he ended unsuccessful love affairs, the ludicrous bouts of heavy drinking, and the costive attention he paid to Frankie Junior suggest that Sinatra formed a carapace of toughness and inscrutability which he passed off as "style."

At one level, Sinatra's conduct is typical of traditional male attitudes in Sicilian/Mafia cultures, and is, more generally, symptomatic of a form of old-fashioned patriarchy. In these circles, when the behavior of an intimate is found wanting and weighed in the balance, the scaffolding of respect and trust that sustains the relationship is blown away. No quarter is offered for defense or exculpation. Severance is nonnegotiable and final. The former intimate is translated into the status of a nonperson. Physical erasure or social isolation follow.

Sinatra's Narcissism

On another level, these are the classic hallmarks of the narcissistic personality. It should be no surprise that achieved celebrity and narcissism are closely related. The achieved celebrity wins fame by reason of his or her accomplishments on earth. But these accomplishments also detach the individual from the earth. Society does not exert a sufficient hold upon the celebrity to guarantee the regulation of desire and emotions. In successfully going beyond general mores and reciprocities and achieving intense acclaim and tributes from fans, the celebrity develops an idealized public face which is projected over all aspects of his or her private and public life. The sense of standing above the world as a role model or figure of popular desire and fantasy, and simultaneously rejecting worldly values since they belong to a less exalted realm, can be psychologically difficult to reconcile. The narcissist may sublimate frustration at being forced back into himself by having providential dreams of social improvement for mankind, or turn to religion as a means of personal salvation. While Sinatra remained a lifelong Catholic, he was not a devoutly religious person. The closest he came to delivering a religious testament to the future is the third disc on *Trilogy* (1980). Part space odyssey, part muddled, vapid, embarrassing, woolly-headed aspiration, the disc is justly described by Sinatra's best music critic, Will Friedwald, as "the most spectacular disaster of his career...[Sinatra] blew it by addressing ideas that were at once too grandiloquent and too stupid" (1996: 356). The vision of the future that it presents is, indeed, piffle, with seemingly universal amity and the end of ignorance and want gracefully descending upon humanity by an act of divine consent.

Meliorist fantasies of general improvement, in fact, often amount to a disguised yearning for immortality, since they presuppose that the defects of this world will be replaced by the bountiful world to come, in which the narcissist can expect, at last, to gain the recognition he or she deserves. But Sinatra's wayward politics suggests that he was unable to adhere to any durable ideal of the good society. To be sure, as he grew older, he became notably more skeptical about schemes of social improvement. Arguably, his respect for the aggression and guile he learnt on the streets of Hoboken expanded. Inversely, his fugitive pleasures delivered diminishing returns. In the final decade of his life, the drinking sessions were often maudlin, lachrymose affairs, as he morosely toasted absent friends. Sinatra remained the center of ceremonies, if no longer, for reasons of apparent dementia, the master. He was still the object of success by which his drinking buddies were urged to measure their own worth. His story was still, in the final analysis, the only relevant *his-story*.

Inasmuch as this is so, it is appropriate to see Sinatra as an orthodox narcissist. The narcissist has problematic relationships with the external world because he places himself at the un-equivocal center of it. This is actually a state of withdrawal because it does not engage with the real external world but replaces real relationships with fantasy substitutes. After achiev-ing celebrity, Sinatra's relationships with women, peers, the Mafia, and presidents possessed a high level of fantasy content. He imagined himself to be irresistible and omnipotent. He saw himself as beyond the rule of law and dealt with any friction of conscience by identifying the common good with the fulfillment of his self-interest.

This is a point of view that requires considerable displays of sociability. Although the narcissist feels fundamentally cut off from worldly life since it fails to measure up to his perceived superior status, he needs company because it provides a forum for the giving of tributes and honors.

Sinatra's appetite for partying and clubbing was legendary. He lived for the nightlife and performing. Habitually, he made it a point of honor to stay up until dawn. His dress sense was generally fastidious and arguably obsessive, which is why I earlier described the mid-1960s episode involving the love beads and Nehru jacket as excruciating. His suit maker was Carroll & Co. of London and Beverly Hills. When he wore a tuxedo he insisted that the shirt cuffs extended no more than half an inch from the jacket sleeve. His trousers were not per-mitted to extend further than the top of his shoe. He tried to avoid sitting down because this wrinkled the cloth. His custom-made shirts were buttoned beneath the crotch. His trouser pockets were carefully arranged: an inside pocket held a white linen handkerchief and little mints, and he carried individually folded tissues in the outer left and a single key on a fob. His paper cash was held in a money clip. He never carried credit cards. He usually wore a pocket handkerchief, generally orange, because it was his favourite colour. Cufflinks were *de rigueur*.

His favored supplier was one Swifty Morgan based in Florida. Although he was oddly averse to some perfumes on women, he usually smelled of *Yardley's English Lavender* or the Spanish cologne *Agua Lavemder Puig*. His closets were meticulously arranged. The state of dishabille was anathema to him, provoking complaints of toxic manners and a lack of self-respect when he encountered it in others. As Tina Sinatra recollects:

> I would marvel at the way things were hung together in categories. Sweaters were folded on shelves; the hats were perched in rows up on the highest shelf; shoes with shoe trees lined the floors. Everything smelled like him. He had a scent and a style and an order to his life always. (Quoted in Zehme 1997: 128)

The process of tipping was likewise primed and orderly. He referred to his tipping as "duking." The term derives from Tin Pan Alley where skimming cash was known colloquially as "dipping his duke in the tambourine." Typically, Sinatra's tips were $100 bills, which is why his behavior on the 1974 tour to Australia when he dispensed $200 bills to all hotel and valet staff was out of character. Perhaps this was his way of diffusing the intense hostility directed at him by the Australian media at this time. According to Tina Sinatra (2000: 228), in his usual social life he gave $100 for a round of drinks and $200 for valet parking. The bills were folded three times into small squares to make it easy to pass them unobtrusively in a handshake. Among Sinatra's tribe, Jimmy Van Heusen, Jilly Rizzo and Hank Cattaeno were delegated the task of carrying and dispensing the money. His generosity was kingly, showering not merely money but also his blessing upon the recipient. Even in old age, Sinatra was concerned with making his mark, with leaving an impression on everyone he encountered.

The Tensions between the Public and the Private Face

George Herbert Mead (1934) held that it is useful to divide the individual between the "I" (the veridical self, or I as I am) and the "Me" (myself as seen by others). The "Me" is assembled from the attitudes and values of the social group and, as such, amounts to the internalization of the generalized other. The healthy individual maintains equilibrium between the "I" and the "Me," so that neither side is permitted to overshadow the other. For the narcissist this equilibrium can often be very precarious indeed. Public acclaim inflates the "Me" so that the "I" feels engulfed and under threat of annihilation. This is especially acute in the case of achieved celebrity. In normal circumstances the I/Me confronts the frailty and vulnerability that is part of the human lot as a mutual partnership. Conversely, for achieved celebrities, the "I" remains locked in the condition of frailty and vulnerability because its true worth is scarcely recognized by the public, while the "Me" is pumped up to appear seductive, radiant, and serenely untouchable.

Moreover, the multiple and conflicting claims of the public introduce schism in the construction of the "Me," so that stable internalization of the generalized other is obstructed. Achieved celebrities are often prey to deeply distressing anxieties and fears about their status with the public. They are more likely to have cosmetic surgery to defend the public's image of the "Me" and to falsify frailty and vulnerability. Statistically, they are also more likely to develop dependence on drugs and alcohol, and resort to psychoanalysis to maintain a public face of equilibrium. The consequence of this is to further undermine the sense of "I as I am." The "I" responds to the public inflation of the "Me" by heightening anxieties concerning annihilation and disappearance. In some cases achieved celebrities resort to regarding the public as a monster that inexorably threatens to devour them. One coping strategy is to withdraw inwardly so as to restore the resources of the "I." Arguably, the classic example of this is Greta Garbo, who withdrew from the limelight at the height of her career for reasons of self-preservation.

Even in the "Dark Ages," when Sinatra's relationship with the public was the most perplexed, his narcissism prevented him from following the Garbo route into voluntary obscurity. Despite declining record sales, film roles and nightclub bookings he continued to court public attention and present himself as the center of the world. He dealt with the disequilibrium between the "I" and the "Me" by two strategies. First, he subjected himself to fulsome self-exculpation. For example, in 1955, during an interview with the writer A. E. Hotchner which touched on the causes behind his career collapse between 1947 and 1953, he observed:

> I did it. I'm my own worst enemy. My singing went downhill and I went downhill with it, or vice versa – but nobody hit me in the throat or choked me with my necktie. It happened because I paid no attention to how I was singing. Instead, I wanted to sit back and enjoy my success and sign autographs and bank the heavy cash. Well, let me tell you, nobody who's successful sits back and enjoys it. I found that out the hard way. You work at it all the time, even harder than when you were a nobody. Enjoyment is just a by-product of success – you get a kick out of it, fine, but the only real fun in being successful is working hard at the thing that brings you success... You hear all the time about guys who showed big promise or who even made it to the top and then suddenly they flub out. Everybody says they must have developed a block or lost their touch or one of the guys at the office was out to get them or whatever: Well, maybe that's just a fancy way of saying the thing I found out: The only guy can hurt you is yourself. (Quoted in Zehme 1997: 218)

In this passage Sinatra denigrates himself only as a pretext to holding that an enlarged, richer personality was given to the world through his suffering, a typical strategy of the narcissistic personality.

Sinatra's second strategy was to construct an inner circle, an allotment of confidantes, to act as a buffer between his exalted state and the fleshy world of the unexalted. As a narcissist, he kept most people at arm's length. When he allowed you into his inner circle and private life he required absolute obedience with his code of honor. Since this code was articulated through example rather than instruction, it was notoriously difficult for others to fathom and apply. Sammy Davis Jr first broke the code in 1959 when, in the course of Jack Eigen's radio show in Chicago, he ventured:

I love Frank and he was the kindest man in the world to me
when I lost my eye in an auto accident and wanted to kill myself.
But there are many things he does that there are no excuses
for. Talent is not an excuse for bad manners... it does not give
you the right to step on people and treat them rotten. This
is what he does occasionally. (Quoted in Quirk and Schoell
1998: 170)

Sinatra punished Sammy for this soliloquy in his customary
fashion. He ceased to speak to him, banned him from attending
any of his public performances, and arranged for MGM to
replace Sammy with Steve McQueen in the film *Never So Few*
(1959). Sammy was forced to make a humiliating public apology
during a TV interview. Only then was Sinatra prepared to relent.

Later in the 1960s and early 1970s, Sinatra broke with Sammy
again. This time the cause was Davis Jr's addiction to cocaine,
which Sinatra abhorred as unmanly. After a long period of
rejection, Sinatra instructed Davis Jr to quit the drug if he
wanted to regain the friendship. Sammy complied and in the
last few years of his life good relations with Sinatra prevailed.

Sinatra's cruelty had a casual, desultory aspect. It could be
articulated thoughtlessly and without apparent premeditation.
It was as if he relished pushing relationships to breaking point
by using abuse and invective to precipitate a crisis in which
loyalty to him would be tested. Sinatra seemed unable to draw
the line between what would pass for ribald banter within his
circle and wounding abuse in public. He was so used to being
king-of-the-castle among his intimate associates that his judgment about the face he showed to these confidantes and the face
he showed to the public was often faulty. The inner cabinet of
Sinatra's tribe was the Rat Pack. With Dean Martin, Sammy
Davis Jr, Peter Lawford and Joey Bishop, between the mid-
1950s and mid-1960s, Sinatra achieved a legend of ensemble
performance that defined male values in consumer culture. In
the words of Quirk and Schoell:

In 1960, Frank and the Rat Pack were the epitome of cool. Men
wanted to be like them, live like them, make love like them: they

118

wanted to stay out all night like they did, bed a different broad whenever they felt like it, and never fear any consequences. They wanted to smoke and drink until it made them sick, throw money around like it was meaningless and feel like irresponsible, irrepressible college boys again. (1998: 184)

The Rat Pack appeared to work for fun, and they earned vast sums of money in so doing. They hinted at limitless sexual licence. They placed themselves on the wheel of conspicuous consumption and unapologetic hedonism. They ridiculed pomposity and formality. Their unvarying attire of evening dress was presented as a mark of respect for the audience. The sentiments of the stage act were generally self-mocking, licentious and occasionally bawdy. Yet there was a code of honor behind Rat Pack repartee. It was based on the male clannish recognition that all five performers had been bruised by faulty relationships with women, drink, bad business deals, and entertainment business double-think. Dean Martin described the Rat Pack as "like the PTA – a Perfect Togetherness Association" (Levy 1998: 186).

Perhaps the best way to think about it is as the public variant of Humphrey Bogart's famous "Fuck You Fund." Throughout his career Bogart was careful with money, always saving a large proportion of his film fees. When a reporter asked him why he was building up large reserves of money instead of enjoying spending it, Bogart replied that the money was going into his "Fuck You Fund." Whenever, a movie mogul tried to inveigle him to play a role he was not interested in, or a director became insolent or boorish, the fund gave Bogart leave to say "Fuck You." It gave him the luxury of walking away from the venture without needing to worry how he could continue to pay the bills. It was the achieved celebrity's charter for doing as he pleased.

Similarly, the Rat Pack "Perfect Togetherness Association" was akin to a performers' combination against the cutthroat entertainment industry. They aimed to maximize control over the stage act, recordings and films, and their earnings from them. The Rat Pack was therefore a form of both financial and emotional protectionism. Its style was to emphasize minimal constraint from the financial and managerial fetters that bound other performers. As such, it was an important precursor to the more informal and personally advantageous financial and artistic deals sought by independent film stars, directors and musicians in the 1960s.

four

THE RAT PACK

The original Rat Pack was not Sinatra's invention. It was an informal, ad hoc association founded in 1955 and presided over by Humphrey Bogart. Lauren Bacall, Bogart's much younger wife, coined the term. On one occasion, in the late night company of Bogart and his friends, she spontaneously described the dishevelled, hung-over, mildewed, supine, middle-aged group as "a god-damn rat pack." Rat Pack headquarters was Bogart's home in Holmby Hills, Los Angeles. It developed its own coat of arms (a rat gnawing on a human hand) and motto: "never rat on a rat." Its members included David Niven and his wife Hjordis, the film director John Houston, the restaurateur Mike Romanoff and his wife Gloria, Judy Garland and her husband Sid Luft, the agent Swifty Lazar, and the songwriter Jimmy Van Heusen.

Sinatra was inducted as a cub member soon after the club was constituted. It celebrated nonconformity, heavy drinking, late night living, practical joking, and the cultivation of a carefree demeanor. It was vaguely permeated with liberal values, but it was primarily a social rather than a political or financial gathering. Bogart's family origins from the Brahmin class of Upper West Side, New York culture conferred upon the Rat Pack an air of sophistication.[1] In some ways it was a West Coast film community version of the writerly Algonquin Round Table that met in New York in the 1920s and 1930s and was devoted to witty conversation, conviviality, clowning, and generous after-hours libation. Although less literary and elitist, the humor and outlook of the Rat Pack owed much to the example of the iconoclasm and urbanity of prewar humorists and cartoonists who were either members of the Round Table or were associated with it, notably Dorothy Parker, E. B. White, Robert Benchley, James Thurber, and S. J. Perelman.

Sinatra's road to membership had been prepared through long standing social connections with Bogart and Bacall. In 1949 Sinatra moved his family from Mary Astor's former estate in Toluca Lake to Holmby Hills, Los Angeles, settling a few blocks from the Bogarts. After his separation from Nancy and the children, he frequently stayed with the Bogarts. Levy contends that Sinatra regarded Bogart as a role model, possessing all the characteristics he coveted: "aloof, profound, world-weary, slightly drunk, slightly sentimental, romantic, tender, tough, loyal and proud" (1998: 28). Bogart acknowledged this identification, declaring that Sinatra viewed Bacall and himself as "parent substitutes" (Levy 1998: 28).

Be that as it may, there is reason to believe that Sinatra's interest in Bacall was carnal as well as convivial. In some accounts, he is alleged to have started an affair with her while Bogart was still alive (Levy 1998: 32–3; Quirk and Schoell 1998: 56). Whatever the truth of the matter, Sinatra evidently relished Rat Pack soirées, especially the hard-bitten attitude displayed to show business impresarios and avaricious film executives, and the carefree mirth-making on which the group thrived. Quirk and Schoell sum up the atmosphere accurately when they write:

> The Rat Pack members all thought they were being unconventional and glamorously out of control, "thumbing their noses at Hollywood" as Bacall put it, but they were also being monumentally silly. (And rather vapid: "We were all terribly young and terribly witty and terribly rich," said fringe member Kay Thompson.) (1998: 61)

When Bogart died on January 14, 1957, Sinatra fell into a depressive stupor, immediately canceling two evening shows at the Copacabana Club in New York. He returned to Los Angeles to mourn. After the funeral, he began escorting Bacall to parties and public functions. His treatment of Bacall, at first solicitous, turned out to be horrible, and is another good example of his narcissism and exacting code of loyalty. By this time he had accepted that he was irrevocably estranged from Ava Gardner. Over the year, his attention to Bacall grew more ardent. He proposed to her on March 11, 1958. The engagement, which was brief, and its explosive aftermath give insight into Sinatra's self-righteousness, elephantine resolve, and violent, unforgiving temperament.

On March 12, while Sinatra was absent in Florida, Bacall attended a party given by Zsa Zsa Gabor for Noel Coward. Swifty Lazar, her agent, accompanied her. During the evening she succumbed to his barrage of questioning and admitted that she and Sinatra were engaged. The gossip columnist Louella Parsons was in attendance and immediately printed the news in the morning newspaper. Sinatra was livid. He appears to have regarded Bacall's announcement as presumptuous. In his mind this fused with an irresistible, unjustifiable conviction that he had been stabbed in the back and publicly humiliated. Needless to say, whatever law Bacall had broken in Sinatra's mind was never articulated during their courtship. Still it was enough to irrevocably set him against her. This in turn raises doubts about the sincerity of his proposal of marriage. Sinatra may have wanted a marriage based upon his lore and thus required Bacall to be utterly subservient. If so, it was rash, since this course of behavior had already proved disastrous with Gardner. It is more likely that his courtship and proposal was an attempt to get over Gardner and that he acted precipitately. Bacall herself remembered that Sinatra's behavior was wildly erratic at this time. Still dwelling on his demoralizing separation from Gardner, he careered between ecstatic highs and noxious lows. He seemed unstable, impulsive, and vulnerable.

At all events, Sinatra summarily dropped Bacall. At first he implied that the rift would be temporary until media interest in the engagement subsided. In response, Bacall reluctantly agreed to cancel planned joint visits to Chicago, New York, and Palm Springs. However, Sinatra, by studied neglect, allowed the two-week separation to drift slowly into absolute severance. He simply, unilaterally and methodically erased her from his life. As Bacall later recalled:

There was no way to understand it. We had been such friends for so long, how could he drop a curtain like this? I was under a permanent cloud then – trying to excuse him to others, pretending I understood – but others had seen this before. No one just drops someone without discussion. It was such a shock. (quoted in Taraborrelli 1997: 278)

Ever after, Sinatra was like a block of ice in her presence. When they met unexpectedly at social functions he refused to acknowledge her. Once, by chance, they encountered one another face to face after a concert and he looked straight through her without, as she recalled, "a flicker of recognition" (quoted in Taraborrelli 1997: 279).

From Holmby Hills to Las Vegas

With Bogart's death the Holmby Hills Rat Pack fell by the wayside. Sinatra began to miss the camaraderie of an inner circle of Hollywood nonconformists. His seduction of Bacall may, in part, be interpreted as an attempt to occupy the place vacated by Bogart. If so, he was also intent on demonstrating that control of the anti-establishment tradition had passed to a new generation, 10 to 15 years younger than the original Holmby Hills Rat Pack. Certainly, the cast of the Rat Pack that he assembled in the 1950s was a new gang of parvenus, far removed from the old-Hollywood celebritariat.

During the filming of *Some Came Running* (1958) Sinatra grew close to his co-star, Dean Martin, who had just broken up his popular partnership with the comedian Jerry Lewis. Born in the Mid-West steel town of Steubenville, Ohio, Martin was more tough-minded and circumspect than Sinatra. Although he appreciated female company, drink, and partying with his buddies, his "pallies" as he called them, he was free of Sinatra's hubris, his inveterate need for an enemy, imagined or real, and his burning desire for legitimacy. Martin was altogether more relaxed with himself. They shared a first generation Italian-American background and held many all-night parties during the film shoot. Sam Giancana and his henchmen were frequent guests at these events, thus providing Sinatra with the gloss of underworld kudos. Martin never shared Sinatra's fascination with the Mafia and tended to avoid accepting any "favors" from Giancana and his associates. Sinatra, of course, relished his role as a superstar and confidante of the mob. He always took vulgar delight in boastfully demonstrating that he was personally connected to men of national influence. It was one reason why he courted John F. Kennedy so assiduously in the late 1950s, and it is also a factor in his friendship with Giancana, Carlo Gambino, Willie Moretti, and other members of the Mafia. Dean Martin was more wary. He understood that the WASP establishment in America is instinctively condescending to parvenu culture, especially if it contains elements from ritually degraded ethnic minorities. As for the Mafia, Martin believed they were fundamentally untrustworthy. He never followed Sinatra's sometime example in glorifying them as romantic Italian-American bandits.

Sammy Davis Jr first met Sinatra when the Tommy Dorsey Band performed in Detroit in 1941. Ten years younger than Sinatra, Sammy was a member of a vaudeville trio which included his father and a veteran stager called Will Mastin. The trio was billed as "Will Mastin's Gang, Featuring Little Sammy." Sinatra was impressed by Sammy's multitalented performing skills. He maintained a casual, desultory relationship, with Sammy regularly attending Sinatra's concerts and receiving the honor of being permitted to attend Sinatra's rehearsals. Sinatra seems to have taken a brotherly interest in Sammy's career. In the late 1940s he secretly persuaded Sidney Piermont, manager of the Capitol Theater in New York, to book the Mastin Gang as an opening act. The trio received a fee that was for them unprecedented – $1,250 per week – again at the behest of Sinatra. In 1954 Sammy crashed his car in Los Angeles and suffered the loss of an eye. Sinatra was a regular visitor to his hospital bedside and was a tower of moral support. Sammy heroically resumed his performing career. Sinatra kept his interest in him, followed his subsequent progress, and helped him out when he could. Gradually, the idea of forming an ensemble act as a counterpoint to his solo career, as a way of having fun with like-minded performers and earning additional income, took root in Sinatra's mind. But first, other elements had to fall into place.

Peter Lawford was a rather dissolute British bit-part player. He was born into an upper-class military family, the son of General Sir Sydney Lawford and May Somerville Bunny. May was an eccentric, headstrong snob. Levy describes her as "a genuinely disturbed woman" and a "megalomaniac" (1998: 59). Like Dolly Sinatra she was extremely ambitious for her only child and solicited movie parts for him in Britain. When he was 14, Lawford gashed his right arm on a glass panel and nearly bled to death. The injury permanently weakened his arm and barred him from military service. As an aside, it is interesting to note that of all the Rat Pack only Sammy Davis Jr and Joey Bishop served in the army. Lawford's damaged arm, Sinatra's perforated eardrum and chronic mastoiditis, and Dean Martin's double hernia disqualified them from participating in the war. The Rat Pack's soldierly air, cultivated on stage and in films like *Ocean's Eleven* and *Sergeants Three* was thus largely fraudulent.

After his injury, doctors advised Lawford to migrate to a warmer climate. The family left for Palm Beach, California and Lady Lawford again entreated film studios to offer Peter roles. He was given little more than walk-on parts in *Mrs Miniver*, *Random Harvest*, *Pilot Five*, and *Sahara*. His breakthrough film was the patriotic *The White Cliffs of Dover* (1944), which led to *Son of Lassie* (1945) and *Good News* (1947). But Lawford was never an A list star. As we shall see, his involvement with the Rat Pack owed more to the important political connections that he later acquired through marriage than his status or talents as a performer.

Sinatra first met Lawford at a party at Louis B. Mayer's house and became a casual friend. He brokered a role for him in the musical *It Happened in Brooklyn* (1947). However, the relationship cooled dramatically when Lawford began dating Ava Gardner. Sinatra behaved in character: he stopped talking to Lawford and refused to acknowledge him in public. It was Lawford's marriage to Pat Kennedy in 1954 that reawakened Sinatra's interest, especially as the 1950s drew to a close and it became evident that Pat's brother and Sinatra's drinking buddy John F. Kennedy intended to run for President.

Joey Bishop was the son of an immigrant machinist, Jacob Gottlieb, and his wife Anna. Again, it is interesting to note in passing that four of the five members of the Rat Pack were first generation Americans: Sinatra and Martin hailed from Italian-American stock, Lawford's parents were British, and Bishop, who changed his name from Gottlieb for career reasons, was the son of Jewish, middle European immigrants. Sinatra first encountered Bishop as a stand-up comedian in New York after the war. He made Bishop his opening act in 1952 when, in the midst of Sinatra's "Dark Ages," the comedian must have offered some much-needed distraction and solace. Bishop's was not a confrontational act. He used laughter to put people at their ease rather than to address difficult political and religious questions. He tried to make audiences like him. With the exception of Dean Martin, Bishop was the only member of the Rat Pack who refused to be ruled by Sinatra. He respected "the leader," knew when to be deferential, but was never obeisant in the manner of Lawford and Davis Jr. As he put it: "I have always respected Frank's moods. I have never walked over to Frank when he's having dinner with someone and sat down uninvited. Which, I think, was another reason why he chose to have me with him" (Levy 1998: 76).

The Biggest Star in America

Between 1957, the year of Bogart's death, and 1963, when the Beatles broke the mould, Sinatra was the biggest star in America. He was successful on so many fronts – in popular music and film, and as nightclub entertainer, society man-about-town, and political fixer – that at times it was difficult for the public to assimilate his achievements. He was simply ubiquitous.

This extraordinary success raises questions beyond talent or accomplishment and points to the representational status of certain celebrities as the condensation of collective desires and wants in a particular epoch. On occasion, celebrity figures emerge who stamp the period with hallmarks of attitude and style and act as axial icons for emulation in popular culture.

127

Arguably, in the field of popular entertainment, Fred Astaire and Ginger Rogers and Greta Garbo occupied this role in the 1930s; Cary Grant and Clark Gable in the 1940s; James Dean, Elvis Presley and Marlon Brando in the 1950s; the Beatles, the Rolling Stones and Bob Dylan in the 1960s; David Bowie, Jack Nicholson and Warren Beatty in the 1970s; Madonna, Michael Jackson, Prince and Tom Cruise in the 1980s, and so on.

What was remarkable about Sinatra is that while it is in the nature of popular culture, especially the music business, to elevate and discard stars willy-nilly, he was *durable*. Unlike other American idols who emerged in the late 1950s, notably Elvis Presley, James Dean, Marilyn Monroe and Marlon Brando, Sinatra was well into his second decade of popular acclaim, having rehabilitated himself after his career slump between 1947 and 1953. Moreover, he continued to occupy the vanguard position in the 1960s as the "chairman of the board." His retirement in 1971 was a half-hearted, unconvincing affair, the end of which only underlined his exalted status in twentieth-century American popular culture. After his comeback in 1973, until failing health forced him off the stage in 1995, Sinatra's tours were kingly affairs, touched in the final years with a piquant quality, as the audience recognized that Sinatra was slowly growing into King Lear.

Why did Sinatra last for so long? At first sight, there is an obvious answer to the question: his versatility transcended that of all of his competitors. On celluloid or vinyl, or acting as a behind-the-scenes political fixer, he excelled. If this was not always recognized by critics, it was, in general, acknowledged by the more important arbiter: the fee-paying public.

But his grip on mass culture also had Freudian roots. For a postwar population that was increasingly disembedded and mobile, Sinatra provided a fixed reference point of achieved authority and success. He symbolized achieved power in an era when the chances of upward mobility for ordinary people multiplied. He was the iconic popular entertainer, the man from Hoboken of all places, who captivated the world. Even when his fame and power elevated him into the stratosphere of American popular culture, ordinary people related to him as if he was still one of them. Arguably, this explains why so many of his fans believed that he was singing and performing *only* for them. Despite the cumbersome paraphernalia of modern celebrity culture – the marketing machine, the teams of cultural inter-mediaries that "shape" the celebrity for the public, the media circus – Sinatra constructed, and for the overwhelmingly greater part of his career maintained, a relationship with his audience that can only be described as *intimate*. This prevailed after the media prosecution case against him that started as early as the late 1940s and centered on his promiscuity, his Mob connections, and his violent nature. The establishment may not have recog-nized him as "one of us," but the exact opposite was true of his staple audience.

It was as if Sinatra's celebrity drew on a psychological need in mass culture for a popular colossus with feet of clay, a figure elevated from the ranks of ordinary people who embodies the conflicting tides and tensions of the masses on the public stage, and who has tasted failure and hardship as well as success and adulation. For his part, despite his wealth, achievement and, in his final years, recurring history of indifferent health, he was incapable of breaking the umbilical cord with the public. When pressed to explain why he continued to tour in spite of failing powers, Sinatra responded that he associated the end of work with death. Most of his close friends, and *all* of the Rat Pack save for Joey Bishop, died before him. "If I stop working, I know I'll be next," he stated (T. Sinatra 2000: 229).

Such a public admission of mortality was rare for Sinatra. He had a phobia about death, and his automatic response to public interest into his ageing process was to be imperious, and affect the swagger of the immortal superstar. His artistically question-able, often risible attempts to remain hip after the 1980s, with *The Present* collection on *Trilogy* (1980), where he awkwardly worked his way through cover versions of *McArthur Park*, *Song Sung Blue* and *Love Me Tender*, and the patchy performances on *Duets* (1993) and *Duets II* (1994), may be read as projects of reinvention. Sinatra did this in the 1950s when he replaced the Big Band sound with more individualistic albums under the orchestration of Nelson Riddle, Billy May and Gordon Jenkins.

He ransacked his Columbia back catalogue by recording his former hits during these years, largely in response to Columbia's decision to release his old recordings to compete with Sinatra's fresher Capitol releases. Sinatra repeated the tactic when he left Capitol for Reprise in the early 1960s (Granata 1999: 147). But throughout his career Sinatra was concerned not only to re-invent former recording glories but to keep up with the times. He did this in the 1960s when he warily recorded "contemporary" music with singles like *Strangers in the Night* (1966), *Downtown* (1966), *Yesterday* (1969) and *Mrs Robinson* (1969). *Duets I* and *II* were moribund attempts, hugely successful it might be added, to bridge the age gap by demonstrating that the octogenarian "Voice" was still hip and that younger performers recognized Sinatra as the maestro.

Mass Idols in Popular Culture

Sinatra was elevated to fame during a transitional stage in celebrity culture. Lowenthal (1961) noted that in the 1920s the conflation of celebrity status with outstanding achievement in the realms of science, the armed forces, the arts and politics was challenged by a new compact: the popular entertainer as mass idol. In the late 1930s, when Sinatra first came to the attention of the public, the idolatry of popular entertainers was widely debated. Sinatra himself was impugned as a seditious mass idol, whose image conjured up a netherworld of sexual license, freedom of expression, and amorality. Interestingly, a decade later Sinatra resorted to similar rhetorical devices to describe the music of Elvis Presley and the rock'n'roll generation. "His kind of music," he remarked acidly, "is deplorable, a rancid-smelling aphrodisiac" (quoted in Miller 1999: 169).

Leaving this aside for the moment, the idolatry of popular entertainers over celebrities from science, the arts, the armed forces and politics that Lowenthal described as commencing in the 1920s became more pronounced after World War Two. True, celebrities like Albert Einstein, Picasso, Dwight Eisenhower, George Patton , Harry S. Truman and John F. Kennedy achieved heroic status in the 1950s and 1960s. But the mass media's colonization of popular culture, especially through television, created an unprecedented demand for new celebrity sensations. It was at this time that the multiplication of celebrities, through talent shows and media publicity stunts, became programmatically organized. After the 1940s the media's readiness to use sensation and spectacle as strategies to increase audience interest produced a strong tendency toward improvising celebrity: that is, constructing mass idol phenomena through the media as a method of generating cultural and financial capital.

The tendency was reinforced by the unparalleled conditions of geographical and social mobility in urban-industrial populations that cut people off from their roots and made them more susceptible to engaging in parasocial relations of intimacy and belonging organized by the mass media. Ever since the writings of the German sociologist Ferdinand Tönnies (1887) we have associated the rise of modern society with the replacement of *gemeinschaft* with *gesellschaft* relations. *Gemeinschaft* (community) relations refer to "affective" ties constructed through enduring relationships with kith and kin. *Gesellschaft* (association) relations are impersonal, calculating, fragmentary, and contractual. They predominate in conditions in which there is an advanced division of labor and high levels of occupational and geographical mobility. In the midst of them one can readily see that individuals may suffer feelings of isolation, alienation and dislocation as they move between different communities and jobs, often in different cities, regions or countries, each with their own specific economic and cultural contexts. In such conditions it might be posited that the imaginary, fantasy virtual relationships constructed between fans and celebrities provide an important source of social integration. They offer a basis for solidarity, recognition and inclusion in the context of wider relationships that are fragmentary, contingent and often unstable. But the integrative function performed by celebrity is also open to abuse.

The age of the celetoid and what Boorstin (1962) called "the pseudo-event" (the ephemeral celebrity image) is the corollary of celebrity culture. The integrative effect of celebrity as a role

131

model for fans is displaced by a culture of distraction in which noteworthy people and events are programmatically constructed by publicists and media spin doctors. In this way sensation is privileged over achievement. A whole genre of popular "reality TV" now caters for this demand through programs like *The Jerry Springer Show, Big Brother, Survivor* and *Pop Idol*. Arguably, the fecundity of the culture of the celetoid and pseudo-event produces a democratizing consequence in how audiences read celebrity. Yet this depends upon a degree of familiarity with the social and economic causes of reality TV and reflexive consciousness about the psychological processes to which audiences are exposed.

Sinatra's elevation coincided with the massive expansion of mass communications. Part and parcel of this was the gradual reduction of celebrity to its crude essence: social and cultural impact. Achieved celebrity became part of the cultural insignia of distinction. This contributed to the erosion of barriers between entertainment celebrity and political celebrity, a process that Sinatra exemplified in his career. As early as 1924, the presidential press agent Edward Bernays decided to "humanize" Calvin Coolidge by inviting a group of Hollywood stars to breakfast with him in the White House. Roosevelt used Sinatra and other stars on his last campaign trail for the presidency to increase his share of the female and youth vote (Wills 1988: 240–2). Ronald Reagan was to become the twentieth-century master at exploiting achieved celebrity on his road to the White House in 1980. However, John F. Kennedy developed similar tactics in the 1950s and 1960s, using his wartime status as a hero and his Hollywood network to glamorize his image against his Republican opponent, Richard M. Nixon.

It would be rash to portray Sinatra as a celebrity who imprinted an insignia upon postwar American culture. His morality was too ambivalent and he was disliked by too many Americans to qualify for that. Still his presence as an idol who survived was generally relished for the reassuring stability that it conveyed. His classic albums in the 1950s (*In the Wee Small Hours, Where Are You?, Only the Lonely*) were artistic triumphs, redefining the experience of popular music as a personally rewarding form of introspection. He alternated them with recordings of assured, unapologetic escapism such as *Come Fly with Me* and *Come Dance with Me*. His film roles were often socially relevant, and indeed, challenged social conventions. For example *From Here to Eternity, Suddenly, The Man with the Golden Arm* and *The Joker Is Wild* dealt with the controversial themes of institutional bullying, political assassination, drug addiction and intimidation which were anathema to the official culture of Eisenhower's America. The ease with which he mixed in the company of John F. Kennedy and later Ronald Reagan while maintaining his usual round of visits to nightclubs and bars in Las Vegas, Los Angeles and New York contrived to create a public image of access.

After the 1960s, a marinated Sinatra developed a new image of masculine cool and public hauteur. It appeared that Sinatra could hobnob with Presidents over lunch and yet dine with Mafia dons in the evening, and escort the world's most alluring actresses and models to nightclubs and bed, with impunity. Perhaps the outward appearance of his lifestyle realized a popular male fantasy of omnipotence. Sinatra's achieved success offered a parable for what hard work and participation in consumer culture could deliver to anyone who dared to venture to be one of the elect. At all events, the popular entertainer, who apart from his career slump between 1947 and 1953, had been at the pinnacle of popular culture since the early 1940s, seemed to be the indestructible point in the heavens against whom all other achieved celebrities in popular entertainment should be judged.

The Outsider

An important tension in Sinatra's personality derived from his *idée fixe* that the popular acclaim he achieved would never translate into acceptance by the establishment. To some degree, the tension was rooted in his narcissism. It was perhaps less a case of him not being good enough for the establishment, as one of the establishment (largely composed, in his view, of stuffed shirts, flunkeys and Champagne Charlies) not being good enough for him. This was certainly more acutely reflected in his personality after the rejection he suffered at the hands of the Kennedys. In part his defection to the Republicans after the late 1960s should be interpreted as an act of overinflated pride vented against his "own" people who he believed had betrayed him. Another motive, alluded to in earlier pages, was his determination to regain his Nevada gambling license following the Cal-Neva debacle.

In his later years, Sinatra's attitude to public life was somewhat bitter and cynical, in marked contrast to the evangelical bonhomie and optimism of his youth. His charitable works were driven by a laudable but sentimental desire to give something back to society. Yet he seemed increasingly uncertain about the kind of society he wanted to support. There was little of the social conscience and radical zeal that marked his political pronouncements in the 1940s, 1950s and early 1960s. However, while he gained pleasure in making donations, especially from his involvement in children's charities, there was an acute feeling of morbid absence in his public life. In his last decade the official honors that he received were sources of gratification, but left him unfulfilled. During the Reagan and Clinton years in which he was a welcome visitor to the White House, he seemed both repelled by the trappings of establishment culture and unable to resist his lust for power and recognition. For Sinatra, the goal of success was always the accumulation of power. The achieved celebrity who has inherited little in the way of social networks upon which to rely must build his own defenses against adversity and his own opportunities for advancement. He must put his faith in his own judgment because there is no one else to depend upon. Of course, Sinatra had his family. In particular Dolly remained a support (and also an occasional cause of embarrassment) until her premature death in an aeroplane accident in 1979. But by then Sinatra had long grown accustomed to relying chiefly on his own judgment in business and personal matters.

Any account of his life must comment on the peculiar degree to which he always lived in his own world. His life in Hoboken was spent in a narcissistic dreamworld of parental adoration, and identification with solipsistic fantasies about the unparalleled opportunities for achieving social impact produced by the combination of mass communications and consumer culture. His formal education ended at 15 and, by his own estimate, he spent no more than 47 days in High School (Clarke 1997: 13). He was an only child who spent many hours of his time at home as a radio addict, entranced by the new musical and comedy routines and captivated by the huge audiences they commanded. He was sensitive to the racially motivated gang hostilities of Hoboken, and regarded his Italian-American background to be both a source of pride and a basis for conflict with racially antagonistic groups. He was a loner, who broke with the Hoboken Four to pursue his career with the Harry James Orchestra and the Tommy Dorsey Band, before leaving both in turn and becoming a solo artist. The amazing success he achieved when he went solo merely reinforced his single-minded streak, for he'd gone solo against the advice of many elder statesmen in the music industry.

The only significant dent Sinatra's career suffered was his troubled relationship with Ava Gardner. Here he self-consciously placed himself as a vulnerable male into the hands of a chosen female equal. There was some positive effect from doing this. For example, Gardner's success in winning him the role of Maggio in *From Here to Eternity* (1953) brought an end to the "Dark Ages" in his career. However, the ultimate consequences of placing his trust in Gardner were dire. He felt unmanned by her infidelities and impotent in the face of her wilful temper. What he regarded to be his honesty in offering her his real self was thrown back in his face as weakness. After the relationship with Ava ended, he became more defensive and wary of exposing his vulnerability and frailty. The American Caesar persona of the gilded leader began to set into stone. Despite all of the adoration from fans, the financial success of his recording and film career and the honors bestowed upon him by government, after Ava, Sinatra fundamentally *withdrew* in emotional terms. The romantic quality in his work, which as Murray Kempton remarked made him believe "that love is eternal and fidelity is a sacred trust" (1998: 13), was increasingly wistful. He wrapped himself up in layers of bravado, fatalism and barroom tough-guy repartee which insulated him from confronting his vulnerability. This most masculine of stars therefore became furtive about trying to cope with his weaknesses and sought to elide them in a show of heroic alcohol abuse, partying, and eerie, unexplicated stoicism.

The break with Ava coincided with a resurgence of his clannish activities and philandering. In all of this he presented his own interests to be paramount, as they never had been fully with Ava. Sinatra plunged into hedonism as a way of avoiding the question of why Ava rejected him, his real self, the vulnerable core behind the public face. The 1950s and early 1960s was the high-water mark of his hedonism and self-absorption. The Rat Pack provided an outlet for gregarious banter and wisecracks, but it was assembled by Sinatra as *his* vehicle and he was in unassailable command over the other performers. "It's Frank's World," as Dean Martin memorably put it. Yet there were unmistakable overtones of self-contempt and desperation about Sinatra's hedonism that the public recognized. This probably enhanced his popularity because it underlined that, despite the trappings of outward success, Sinatra was all too human. Thus, his strenuous attempt to negate his vulnerability paradoxically had the effect of exposing it. Only with his marriage to Barbara Marx in 1976 did the 61-year-old Sinatra make substantial concessions from his hedonistic, self-centred lifestyle.

In many of his film roles, Sinatra played an outsider adrift from the values of both middle America and the WASP establishment. One thinks of John Barron, the disillusioned would-be assassin in *Suddenly*, Frankie Machine, the junky card-dealer in *The Man with the Golden Arm*, and Dave Hirsh, the realist writer in *Some Came Running*. In his career, the quintessence of this was realized in the Rat Pack days. At this time, Sinatra, the twice married father of three, outwardly offered Americans an extremely congenial image of consumer contentment – *Nice 'n' Easy*, as his 1960 Capitol album styled it. Inwardly, he remained unsure of his place in American society and beset by an overwhelming sense of rootlessness. Sinatra's career is characterized by a strong sense of yearning for belonging and an equally powerful converse skepticism that genuine recognition would ever be his lot.

Without doubt, the Rat Pack reflected these concerns and further elaborated them in their stage act and film work. In 1957, Sinatra was 42. The ages of the other members of the Rat Pack in this year were Dean Martin, 40; Joey Bishop, 39; Peter Lawford, 34; Sammy Davis Jr, 32. For men and women of his parents' generation, Sinatra, Martin and Bishop would have been regarded as "mature," if not well advanced into middle age. Yet the late 1950s was a moment when the concept of maturity was radically revised, at least for the strata in American society with money. The reinvention of self, which was a staple of American culture from revolutionary times and was institutionalized in the nineteenth century in the notion of the Western frontier, became medicalized. A combination of callisthenics, cosmetic surgery and diet offered achieved celebrities the elixir of youth. The middle-aged adolescence of the Rat Pack answered to the expectations explosion of the late 1950s, in which the real wages of most workers increased dramatically and the consumer goods market mushroomed. The buttoned-up, watchful attitudes of the Truman/Eisenhower era were challenged by the new sovereign right of pleasure-seeking, self-expression, and personal enjoyment.

The Rat Pack Culture of Escapism

The Rat Pack symbolized the figure of the guiltfree adult consumer determined to enjoy life in the midst of Cold War anxiety. The conflict between the two systems – capitalism and communism – produced the Korean War of 1950–3 and the Vietnam War, in which America was involved for 20 years between 1955 and 1975.[2] Against the threat of global annihilation, the Rat Pack offered a human-scale reply of guilt-free escapism that used ribaldry and music to assuage anxiety. However, the stage persona they cultivated was based on an aura of cool that militated against identification with the audience. The audience was often patronized as mere squares. For all of its back-slapping approval of the common man, the Rat Pack act made a virtue of their ultimate superiority. Unapologetic male sexism was bred in the blood and bone of the act, as was tolerance for hard drinking, fooling around, and hedonism. Mia Farrow cited this as a reason for the collapse of her marriage. "All they know how to do," she said of the Rat Pack and other members of Sinatra's tribe, "is tell dirty stories, break furniture, pinch waitresses' asses and bet on their horses" (quoted in Weiner 1991: 268).

Racism was outwardly vilified, although regrettably Sinatra and Martin frequently exploited the poverty of the racist imagination by using Sammy Davis Jr as the butt of their onstage jokes. They called Sammy "Smokey" and the nickname was clearly not a reflection on his nicotine addiction. There was certainly no tokenism about Sammy Davis Jr's membership of the troupe. His talents for singing, dancing and impersonation were extraordinary. All the same, he was the circumscribed black man in the Rat Pack, a status which allowed Sinatra and Martin to playfully highlight his color while piously denigrating racism. Upward mobility was championed and old money vilified, although there was always a latent wish for acceptance by the establishment. Later this was evidenced by Sinatra's switch from the egalitarian, reformist ideals of the Democratic Party to the heroic individualism and sentimental communitarianism of Reagan's Republican Party, and Sammy Davis Jr's black bourgeois discomfort with black militantism (Quirk and Schoell 1998; 323–4). Self-consciously and presentationally, the Rat Pack regarded themselves as representing a break between the inward-looking, square values of prewar America and a more relaxed, self-deprecating, meritocratic future.

But the Rat Pack did not identify with either the establishment or their audience and they were quick to condemn criticism of their talents and values. They were outsiders by virtue of the first generation immigrant status of the four white performers. This was reinforced by Sammy Davis Jr's color and the treatment of him by the others as an equal. Mixed race acts were relatively rare during this period. In the 1950s and early 1960s, there is no parallel for a star of Sinatra's stature working over a prolonged period on stage, film and recordings with a person of color. Sinatra's example in fostering multiracial tolerance should not be underestimated. The outsider status of the Rat Pack was redefined by them as a basis for arrogance. By demonstrating cool in the face of middle American racial intolerance, myopia and self-satisfaction, they challenged stereotypes. They regarded themselves as setting the benchmark of cool not simply with respect to dress, but also to racial, sexual and party politics.

The act was full of quips against the wayward attention or inebriation of the audience. Sinatra's monologue in the *Sinatra at the Sands* album of 1966 berates a member of the audience for leaving before he is finished. "The way you're walking," declares Sinatra, "8 to 5 you don't get there in time!" At another moment, when the audience doesn't get one of his jokes, Sinatra quips, "Listen, I'll hold it up till you get back buddy. I'll *linger*." This camaraderie and the collusion of the audience in their own castigation was of course part of the vaudeville ethos that Sinatra grew up with in the 1920s and 1930s. However, often, perhaps *too* often during the Rat Pack years, it was unclear whether the performers were laughing with the audience or *at* them. Sinatra and his colleagues on stage and elsewhere frequently gave the impression that they were beset by a herd of squares.

Paradoxically, their self-absorption prevented them from keeping up with changes in the wider popular culture. Martin and Sinatra, in particular, were stubbornly unable to recognize the value of the new pop and rock entertainers of the 1960s. The style of the new acts, with its emphasis on authenticity, honesty, idealism and spontaneity, seemed to be the antithesis of the carefully contrived barroom witticism and sarcastic repartee that the Rat Pack favored. It is as if the Rat Pack saw themselves and their audience as part of a fallen world in which idealism had no place, save for the artificial sphere of party politics, and youth culture as the recrudescence of primitivism. Sinatra could cajole his colleagues to sing for John F. Kennedy's Democrat Convention and lend a hand on the campaign trail. He could pretend, somewhat implausibly, to approve of Elvis Presley, recently released from his army duty, in a contrived ABC TV special, called *Welcome Home Elvis* (May 12, 1960). But the values he exemplified were the whisky-soaked, sentimental, old-style manly virtues of stoicism, possessive individualism, and tribal loyalty. This was an inclusive philosophy of entertainment that often marginalized the audience.

The perfect example of this is supplied at the end of their performing life together. Sinatra devised the "Together Again" tour in 1988 as a way both of rekindling the glory days of the Rat Pack and of rehabilitating Dean Martin. By this time, Martin was well into retirement and had still not recovered from the death of his son Dino Jr in an aeroplane crash in 1987. The tour was actually built around a depleted Rat Pack, consisting of Sinatra, Martin, and Sammy Davis Jr. Peter Lawford had died in 1984; and Joey Bishop had parted company with the group in the 1970s following an unpublicized altercation with Sinatra – aside from a couple of benefit performances he never worked with the Rat Pack again. Dean Martin was tepid about the whole Together Again project. He saw himself as too old to clown around for the audience again and was still depressed by the death of his son. But he succumbed to Sinatra's well-meaning badgering that the tour would be a riot of fun, and therapy for him. Of all the Rat Pack, Martin possessed the keenest sense of irony, both with respect to his own position as a mass idol and to the place of the Rat Pack legend in American popular entertainment. He regarded the glory days as memorable times, but he never invested them with the sacred significance that Sinatra, especially in his later years, cultivated. For Martin, the public often seemed to be stupid, overready in both their acclaim and disapproval, and all too easily taken in by the blandishments of the media and pop promoters. He did not much regret this trait in public attitudes, because by exploiting it he became a rich man. But he saw no *a priori* virtue in the audience, and no nobility in performance. For Dean, entertainment was just a *business*.

All of this came to a head in the misconceived Together Again tour. At the first show in the Oakwood Coliseum Arena, Martin was uneasy and seemed easily distracted. There were problems with the sound system and he pleaded that he wanted to go home, to the laughter of the crowd. Nick Tosches takes up the story thus:

At one point, his mood seemed suddenly to change. He looked long and hard at the faceless sea beyond the stage. What the fuck was he doing here, and who the fuck were these people? He took a final drag from his cigarette and flicked the burning butt into the crowd. (1992: 437–8)

After the show, Sinatra tore into him for insulting the audience and urged him to display more respect next time. Martin was nonplussed and quit the tour one day later in Chicago. Liza Minelli was drafted in to replace him and the tour was hastily rechristened the "Ultimate Event."

Sinatra's anger with Martin derived from the *public* exhibition of celebrity hauteur. In private Sinatra could be equally rude to fans. Taraborrelli recounts an incident that occurred in 1991 at Sir Harry's Bar in the Waldorf Astoria Hotel in New York. The 76-year-old Sinatra was having a drink at about five in the morning with staple members of his tribe, Jilly Rizzo and Steve Lawrence, when a fan approached him to ask for an autograph. Taraborrelli reports that Sinatra responded in hostile terms: " 'Don't you see I'm on my own time here?' Frank shouted at him. 'You asshole. What's wrong with you?' The fan then said something to Frank that the singer didn't like. Sinatra lunged at him. Lawrence and Jilly held him back as the terrified fan ran off" (1997: 647).

Of course, Sinatra, like Martin, could also often be very patient with importunate fans who invaded his private life. But the incident at the Waldorf Astoria was not isolated. Sinatra was often brutally dismissive of fans. Nor did his fury with the press abate. He was capable of deeply offensive behavior that smacked of a persecution complex. One of the most widely cited examples is also the most odious. At a pre-inaugural party in 1973 he became incensed with the *Washington Post* columnist Maxine Cheshire, and verbally assaulted her thus: "Get away from me, you scum. Go home and take a bath ... You're nothing but a two-dollar cunt. You know what that means, don't you? You've been laying down for two dollars all your life." He made the declaration in full view of many witnesses and climaxed by thrusting two dollar bills into her wine glass with the taunt:

"Here's two dollars, baby, that's what you're used to" (quoted in Weiner 1991: 269).

Sinatra's friends made excuses that he was inebriated and that Cheshire had treated him unfairly in her reports. But again, it is not an isolated incident and reinforces the point that belligerence figured as strongly as an element in his attitude to the public as generosity.

The Ultimate Capitalist Entertainers

One may put it provocatively and submit that the Rat Pack was the exemplary capitalist stage-act of 1950s/1960s American consumer culture. Their work celebrated civil rights, but as a way of increasing involvement in consumer culture and self-expression rather than to challenge the pivotal political and cultural values of the system. They were richly sarcastic about officialdom, but dulled any critical impulse with a sodden, enveloping exterior of barroom patriotism. Of course, they believed in "America the Beautiful," for hadn't America given them opportunities and a lifestyle undreamt of by their parents? However, no political alternative emerged from their work, save for a narrow concern to increase the artistic autonomy and financial rewards of entertainers by gaining a higher percentage of box office gross.

They participated in an entertainment system that they knew from experience disfigured talent and ambition by subjecting both to monetary ends and commodifying art. Admittedly, Reprise records, which Sinatra founded in 1961, sought to increase artistic control and financial reward for performers on the label.[3] It was one of Sinatra's most successful ventures, attracting performers of the calibre of Dean Martin, Sammy Davis Jr, Bing Crosby, Rosemary Clooney, and Trini Lopez. Of course, Sinatra was the leading performer on the label. Nonetheless, Reprise was never seriously interested in transforming either society or the record industry, by for example criticizing the Vietnam war or abandoning the corporate business structure. In 1963 Sinatra sold two-thirds of the company to Warner Brothers for $3.5 million. He obtained one-third of Warner Brothers Records and Warner Reprise prospered to become WEA (Warner-Elektra-Atlantic), one of the top five conglomerates in the pop music business.

What comes through most forcefully is the dependence of the Rat Pack on the capitalist values of competitive individualism and accumulation. Their charity work continued the long tradition of American philanthropy, especially in providing more opportunities for the achievement of individuals from underprivileged backgrounds. They were vociferous critics of racism and class injustice. But this was at a moment when it was *chic* to act thus, and Sinatra in particular became more reactionary and dismissive of welfare programs in old age.

The ensemble played to a popular prejudice in American life, namely that the wrong people are in control of many areas of the federal government. There is a prelapsarian optimism, not to say naivety, about this, which is again very American, since it renews the principle of reinvention by holding that one can bring "virtuous," "untainted" people to run the country through an effort of common will. But in the case of the Rat Pack, this is balanced with a strong conservative and sarcastic conviction that the essentials in society will never change. Nothing in the Rat Pack school of politics suggests that they were in favor of equality and the establishment of genuine dialogic relationships between social formations. What they wanted was meritocracy and a hierarchy that was less hidebound than the WASP ladder of power, but which nonetheless recognized the importance of social position, respect, and patriotism. For example, Sinatra and Martin were publicly critical of the counterculture, especially the anti-Vietnam War movement. For his part, Sammy Davies Jr rejected the militant Black Power movement and favored instead a corporatist solution to racism based on partnership between black leaders and the official representatives of whites. The Rat Pack was often very dismissive of government, but all of them favored order.

Garry Wills (1999) argues that the American attitude to central government can be explained by the fact that the original colonies possessed no central organ of expression. They were founded on different constitutional and economic bases, with markedly contrasting religious and cultural traditions. The American attitude, writes Wills, is "that government is a necessary evil, should be kept to a minimum; and that legitimate social activity should be provincial, amateur, authentic, spontaneous, candid, homogeneous, traditional, popular, organic, rights-related, religious, voluntary, participatory and rotational" (1999: 17–18). This captures the idiom of Rat Pack politics and performance very well. They cherished independence from both highbrow and lowbrow opinion, preferring instead their own version of meritocratic common sense. The latter valorized freedom, civil rights, free speech, and the unfettered pursuit of individual pleasure. At its most lurid it was easy to caricature as the conflation of hedonism with self-expression.

Outwardly, the play ethic cultivated by the Rat Pack was very pronounced. The fraternity house late night carousing, drinking to excess, sexual abandon, gambling, and wheeling and dealing are the ineradicable mark of the Rat Pack during this period. Conversely, it is easy to overlook that the ensemble worked extremely hard, regularly performing twice a day and combining the stage act with an intensive program of filming. Moreover, behind the camaraderie and clowning there was a coherent business plan informing all of their activities. Sinatra financed the first Rat Pack film, *Ocean's Eleven* (1960), and rewarded Peter Lawford, who had bought the screenplay for $10,000, with a fee of twice that amount, plus a salary of $3,000 per week during production and one-sixth of the gross. Dean Martin received $150,000 and Sammy Davis Jr $125,000 – enormous fees by the standards of the day. *Sergeants Three* was coproduced by Sinatra's Essex subsidiary and Dean Martin's Claude Productions. Davis Jr received a fee of $75,000 plus 7 percent of the gross. *Four for Texas* was coproduced by Sinatra, Martin, and the director Robert Aldrich. Sinatra produced the last Rat Pack movie, *Robin and the Seven Hoods – or Who Maid Marian?* (1964).

What comes through most cogently is that the Rat Pack films and stage act were designed to maximize financial independence and protect artistic control from movie moguls, promoters, and managers. The Rat Pack challenged the values of the old Tin Pan Alley and the Hollywood studio system of managing celebrities to give much greater freedom and financial reward to performers. It signified what proved to be a false dawn in the history of popular entertainment: the achieved celebrity as unencumbered artist/playboy, freed of the moral and business constraints that conditioned the behavior of previous generations of artists and bohemians in the age of industrial society.

Life on the Road and at Rancho Mirage

Sinatra was never interested in being full-time recording tycoon. He enjoyed his playboy existence and, in particular, life on the road too much. Indeed, for Sinatra, touring was a way of life. In the twilight of his career, the tours were marshaled with military rigor. In later life his habit of partying into the early hours receded. Although he continued to relish performing, the process of concert performance was very different from the tour bus routine that he experienced in his twenties with the Harry James Orchestra and the Tommy Dorsey Band. By the mid-1960s, when he was performing in the US his personal plane would drop him at the local airport a few hours before the concert, and after the performance it immediately transported him back to his Palm Springs estate or New York apartment. For overseas performances he would hire a floor of the best hotel and ensconce himself and his tribe in secluded residence for the duration of his concert commitment. His offstage contact with fans was minimal, except in staged public relations events like press conferences.

Of his many homes, he preferred to relax at his Rancho Mirage estate in Palm Springs, where he was generally a late riser (usually 2.30 p.m.). Here he devoted himself to painting, reading newspapers, watching television (the game shows *Jeopardy!* and *Wheel of Fortune* were favorites), and playing with his train set.[4] The routine was punctuated with Monday night meals in Palm Springs with his cronies, or lavish dinner parties requiring the employment of up to 25 additional staff. Regular visitors included Gregory Peck and his wife, Chuck Connors, Merv Griffin, Robert Wagner and Jill St John, Roger Moore, Bobby

Marx (the son of Barbara Sinatra, his third wife) and, of course, his children and grandchildren. Sinatra's relaxation mirrored his work in being conducted almost exclusively on his own terms. As he grew older and his powers of concentration and physical energy were impaired, he ignored medical advice to reduce his drinking. He could be abrupt and cutting with friends, especially when he lost interest in socializing. At dinner parties at Rancho Mirage, to the understandable consternation of his wife, Barbara, he would frequently abandon guests after dinner to repair to his train-set room and his own world.

An important part of the Rat Pack is influence on American popular culture centered on their role in changing the iconography of style and hedonism. Some of the motifs they employed, notably their obsession with *couture*, informality and group language, were borrowed from jazz circles that operated with a longstanding division between cool and square values. To some degree, Sinatra and the Rat Pack succeeded in transplanting these motifs from jazz clubs into casino auditoriums and thus rendered them acceptable to white middle American audiences. In this sense, the Rat Pack was not so much an original invention as a representation of deep-rooted values of hedonism and free expression developed in subterranean black avantgarde circles and transplanted into the novel spatial settings of white-dominated entertainment venues. In this respect, a crucial element was the emergence of casino venues which catered for white out-of-towners seeking accommodation, food, fun and entertainment on one site. The paradigmatic example, of course, was Las Vegas.

Vegas

Fittingly, Las Vegas, and especially the Sands Hotel, emerged as the focal point of the Rat Pack's activities. America's "sin city" was partly financed from Mafia funds obtained through narcotics trafficking. It is an essential part of its mythology that the city did not emerge by caprice, but through an act of invention. In the Book of Genesis the wickedness of Sodom and Gomorrah is avenged by fire and brimstone. In mid twentieth-century America, Las Vegas was invented as both an affront to the gods and a spectacular business venture. Sinatra's sometime associate Bugsy Siegel and Siegel's boss, Meyer Lansky, the business brain behind Mafia Inc., were key underworld figures involved in the rise of the city. Denton and Morris (2002) show the position of Las Vegas as a sort of alluring antistructure in American culture, seducing millions of visitors every year with its promise of fast living, gambling, and easy sex. Las Vegas established a postwar benchmark in the nation for political intrigue, business chicanery, sexual license, and organized crime. In urban terms, it symbolized the informalization of American popular culture and the antiutopian realization that corruption was an essential ingredient in American power.

This was the milieu in which the Rat Pack thrived and their stage image crystallized. As the film actress Shirley MacLaine, one of many "honorary" female members of the Rat Pack, recalls:

> When we made pictures at the same time as [the Rat Pack] was appearing in Vegas, there was an energy there that has never been duplicated since. Two shows a night, seven days a week, for three months – while shooting a picture. Granted these pictures were not award winners…but the spontaneous humor on the stage and set was unparalleled. The director never knew what was going to happen or how a scene would be played on a given day. But it didn't matter. (Quoted in Clarke 1997: 188–9)

The Rat Pack savored the image of the playboy. Sexually liberated, upwardly mobile but still streetwise, physically vigorous, sworn enemies of pomposity and organization man didacticism, they personified a mythical, yet extremely powerful version of masculine identity in consumer culture. At its nucleus was the idea that fame and success could be attained through play. The American vaudeville tradition experimented with this theme and, as such, was a largely unacknowledged influence on the Rat Pack. However, few vaudeville performers were as open in their whisky-soaked priapism or nonconformity as the Rat Pack. Sinatra's mantra was "fun with everything and I mean **fun**" (quoted in Zehme 1997: 87, emphasis in original). The same sentiment had been beguiling in the vaudeville period, but lower real wages combined with a much smaller consumer market and restricted leisure time prevented it from being embraced as a popular lifestyle.

By the late 1950s the situation was transformed. Economic reconstruction and the expansion of civil rights created unprecedented opportunities for thousands of people to experience rapid upward mobility. For these people the prospect of not working as hard as their fathers, earning much greater sums of disposable income and expanding their leisure and tourism activities became a reality. They responded positively to Sinatra's philosophy of "fun with everything." Even more so because immediate gratification was permeated by the anxiety that the chances of enjoying fun might be at a premium, not so much for economic reasons as by reason of the nuclear threat of the Cold War. There is a distinct edgy quality to popular entertainment at this time, as if performers and audiences believed they were living on borrowed time.

The Rat Pack adapted (mainly from jazz circles) and begat a vocabulary which was designed instantaneously to sort the socially and physically inept, the squares, from the cool (Shaw 1968; Zehme 1997):

A gas:	a good situation
A gasser:	a very good person
A Bunter:	a very wearisome person
A Nowhere:	the most wearisome person
A Harvey:	a square
A Beard:	an alibi
A Clyde:	a utility word, acquiring definition circumstantially. Thus, "Let's give it another clyde" at the roulette wheel means let's give it another spin; "He's a real clyde" means he should be avoided
Bombsville:	a major failure
Scramsville:	a place to which Bunters, Nowheres, Harveys, and Clydes are repatriated
Endsville:	a termination point, usually applied at the end of the evening
A little hey-hey:	sexual congress

A fink:	a loser
A Charley:	a pal; but also a social embarrassment as in the phrase "Let's lose Charley"
A chick:	a desirable female
Bird:	another utility word, acquiring definition circumstantially, which succeeded "clyde" in Sinatra's vocabulary

The language is, of course, a badge. To possess the language is to share in a narrative of belonging that establishes immediate boundaries with the rest of the world. It is an important sign of the elect: a mark of cool and a curse to the world of the squares. One does not understand the special impact of the Rat Pack in the late 1950s and early 1960s unless one appreciates the degree to which they regarded themselves as representing the *nouvel homme* in consumer culture. This was reflected in the jocose assault against seriousness, which was such a prominent feature of the Rat Pack's act. Although their patriotism and support for a meritocracy was never in doubt, it was often conveyed via strong antiestablishment sentiments. It was also evident in their unapologetic hedonism and hatred of cant and bigotry. By the mid-1950s the public regarded them as personifying the central values of the *Playboy* male.

The *Playboy* Generation

The first issue of Hugh Hefner's men's magazine *Playboy* was published in November of 1953, advertising the first, full-color print of Marilyn Monroe in the nude. As Hefner explained in the original editorial, the magazine was not devoted to the high affairs of state. It presented itself as the antidote to the worries of the age of the atom bomb. In addition to photographs of naked women, the magazine offered male readers cutting-edge fiction, provocative nonfiction, cartoons, and pictorial features on male fashion, jazz, food and drink, cars, and stereos. *Playboy* was the house magazine for the upwardly mobile American male who wished to distance himself from the privations and self-discipline of the wartime mentality and enjoy the profligacy of consumer culture. In the April 1956 edition of the magazine, a staff writer, Ray Russell, penned a manifesto for playboys:

> What is a playboy? Is he simply a wastrel, a ne'er-do-well, a fashionable bum? Far from it: he can be a sharp-minded young business executive, a worker in the arts, a university professor, an architect or engineer. He can be many things, providing he possesses a certain *point of view*. He must see life not as a vale of tears, but as a happy time; he must take joy in his work, without regarding it as the be-all and end-all of living: he must be an alert man, an aware man, a man of taste, a man sensitive to pleasure, a man who – without acquiring the stigma of the voluptuary or the dilettante – can live life to the hilt. This is the sort of man we mean when we use the word *playboy*.

Already – well before Harvey (1989) made the concept of *flexible accumulation* fashionable – the Hefner-endorsed version of the playboy was depicting a male who could be "many things," respectful of work but also hedonistic, "alert," and ready to "live life to the hilt." The crucial characteristic of playboy status was the indefinable "certain point of view." This was composed of a mixture of elements: an inclination to hedonism, ultimate sufferance of family responsibilities, adoption of a perpetually optimistic, positive outlook, a capacity to move readily between formal and informal codes of behavior, an acceptance of fate, a respect for money, and a refusal to allow the physical ageing process dominion over one's pleasure-seeking instincts. All of these elements figured prominently in the ethos of the Rat Pack and served to separate their version of cool common sense from highbrow and lowbrow precedents.

The *Playboy* outlook was deeply influenced by the new promise of science, medicine, and technology. To *Playboy* man the atomic and space age seemed to signify an absolute break with the world of his parents. It presented men and women with a *homo duplex* image of the future. On one hand, the prospect of exciting, revolutionary emancipation from most of the cares of want and illness that had hitherto been the lot of humanity; on the other hand, the sobering prospect of nuclear meltdown. Not surprisingly, the *Playboy* generation flirted with fatalism, albeit always balanced with a none too subtle touch of spikey exceptionalism. The magazine's cartoons frequently displayed a gallows humor. At the same time, the magazine's readiness to interview political leaders was partly an acknowledgment that readers wanted to overcome the impotence they felt in the face of the immense powers released by technology, science, medicine, and politics. Not for them the status of the *passive* citizen that belonged to the previous generation. The *Playboy* generation was made up of *active* citizens who regarded knowledge as power and ascribed authority as inherently questionable. Unlike their fathers' generation, *Playboy* readers would not allow war to creep up stealthily behind their backs. They would employ knowledge and determination to be one step ahead of the game. Fundamentally, they would take all necessary measures to ensure that they always came out on top. Winning was always the indispensable idiom of playboy status, later exemplified in the 1960s with the cinematic version of James Bond.

The *Playboy* generation was also deeply marked by Joseph McCarthy's crusade against Communists and Communist sympathizers in the US. The motif of a powerful external threat – from Germany and then the Soviet Union – was a carryover from the war years and the immediate postwar period, and it saturated American culture at this time. In his famous speech in Wheeling, West Virginia, delivered on the anniversary of Lincoln's birthday in 1950, McCarthy embodied American anxieties in the most devastating way for the national psyche. He posited a hidden enemy within:

> While I cannot take the time to name all the men in the State Department who have been named as active members of the Communist Party and members of a spy ring, I have here in my hand a list of 205 – a list of names that were made known to the Secretary of State as being members of the Communist Party and who nevertheless are working for and shaping policy in the State Department. (Quoted in Herman 2000: 99)

American distrust of government, which reaches back to the American Revolution and the *Federalist Papers,* was greatly panicked by this allegation. The public disquiet engendered by McCarthy's speech derived not from the assertion of Communist infiltration, but from the allegation that the *State Department* was awash with Communists. It was as if American openness and fair dealing were being covertly and ruthlessly exploited by alien forces bent upon nullifying liberty. The punchline of America as mug is not palatable to a nation founded on the valor of individual conscience and the art of personal reinvention. McCarthy made the American public feel not only at risk from enemy spies, but also embarrassed by their open-hearted naivety. *The Manchurian Candidate* parodies the speech with the Red-baiting Senator John Iselin, played by James Gregory, drunkenly alleging Communist subversion to a thunderstruck press conference. Greil Marcus (2002: 75) proposes that the film inimitably condenses American paranoia, born perhaps out of an innate and unapologetic insularity, a migrant fear that there is always someone smarter, better connected, more powerful out there. Be that as it may, I think it is Sinatra's greatest film performance, imparting both impenetrable sorrow at the myth of the American dream and visceral hunger for renewal.

Fort Sinatra

The Rat Pack was Sinatra's fort. If I might be permitted to coin a phrase in this book, allow me to rechristen the Rat Pack: Fort Sinatra. What do I mean by this? It allowed him to be the publicly acknowledged leader of a new middle-aged group that epitomized the novel, candid, uncondescending values of cool. By opposing flummery and humbug, they were the counterparts of the British "angry young man" movement. Certainly, both excoriated the traditional values of docility, unquestioning obedience, and knowing one's place. In principle, the Rat Pack valued social inclusion and extending participation. In reality it was a defensive, remarkably conservative ensemble clinging on to the traditional ascendancy of male power and competitive individualism, and unable to articulate a political philosophy that espoused anything more meaningful than self-expression and the pursuit of individual hedonism. They reinforced the values of the newly emerging consumer culture with their emphasis on personal advancement, conspicuous consumption, patriotism, and Dionysian rewards in the sphere of leisure. They were fiercely dismissive of new genres of popular entertainment, especially pop and rock'n'roll music.

Sinatra famously sought to both slight and exploit Elvis Presley in the celebrated ABC TV special *Welcome Home Elvis* (1960). The show was Presley's first appearance after completing his army service, and Sinatra clearly seeks to use it as a vehicle for demonstrating the sophistication of the Rat Pack in comparison with the hick talent of the Tennessee upstart. Presley appears in army uniform at the start of the special but is immediately displaced by Sinatra, who sings his own numbers, engages in a duet with Nancy Sinatra, and frolics in various routines with Joey Bishop, Sammy Davis Jr and Peter Lawford for most of the show. Presley returns for the finale, this time dressed in a tuxedo, in which he sings *Witchcraft*, while Sinatra repays the tribute with a hammy version of *Love Me Tender*. The subtext of the special is a contrived attempt to demonstrate the superiority of "The Voice" over the "new wave." In the event, it misfires, exposing for young fans the troglodyte cool of Sinatra and his cohort against Presley's unpretentious self-assurance.

Rat Pack braggadocio and display of conspicuous consumption dated quickly after the mid-1960s, under the influence of feminism, militant black power, and the counterculture. For a while, Sinatra and his colleagues became oddly embattled figures. Sinatra continued to release successful recordings and films. To some degree he extended his cinematic range with the *Tony Rome* series of detective films (*Tony Rome*, 1967, *Lady in Cement*, 1968) but his film career was clearly running down. Between 1955 and 1965 he starred in 24 movies. Between 1965 and 1980 he starred in just seven, ending his film career with *The First Deadly Sin* (1980). In this sombre movie Sinatra plays Edward X. Delaney, a New York Detective Sergeant with an ailing, bedridden wife (Faye Dunaway) who, months away from retirement, dedicates himself to the obsessive pursuit of a serial killer. Dunaway's portrayal of a character suffering from a chronic degenerative illness, and the sense of encroaching mortality that Sinatra imparts in his performance as Delaney, invest the film with a bleak, desolate tincture. It is the only screen role in which Sinatra plays an obviously elderly man, and it provides a peculiarly gloomy denouement to his film career.

Sinatra enjoyed recording and touring success in the 1960s. However, he also gradually faded from occupying the cutting edge in popular music. The pop and rock formats did not suit his style of intonation and he bridled at the influence of the counterculture in making a virtue of informal dress, noncompetition, and anti-Vietnam sentiment. Although he had hits with pop songs, he was a square peg in a round hole during the 1960s cultural revolution.

His unease with the shift in the ground was one reason for his "retirement" from the stage in 1971. Sinatra's triumphant return to the stage two years later makes the retirement gesture now look like a plea for winning new levels of tribute. It was as if by retiring at full power, Sinatra was inciting the audience to beg him to make a comeback. If so, it would be consistent with the treatment of individuals who, he believed, had shown disrespect in his private life. He would always turn his back on them in a final way and force them to plead to be readmitted into his life. Be that as it may, Sinatra's half-hearted, counterfeit retirement revived his legend. When he recommenced touring in 1973 he did so as the triumphant Voice who had outlived the counterculture of the 1960s and returned to reclaim his patrimony. It must be granted that nostalgia was a large part of Sinatra's appeal in the last 22 years of his concert career. He was still a formidable singer, but his claim to be important to the direction of popular music was bogus.

As we have seen, his performances and rerecordings of old standards were often impeccable, but with one or two exceptions his efforts to break new ground were unsuccessful. His comeback was accompanied by a new album, *Ol' Blue Eyes Is Back* (1973). Will Friedwald expresses disappointment at the album, describing it as "the odd combination of the generally infantile songs of Joe Raposo with the often grandiose orchestrations of Gordon Jenkins" (1996: 460). According to Friedwald the only worthwhile albums that Sinatra recorded after 1973 are *The Main Event* (1974), *Trilogy* (1980), and *She Shot Me Down* (1981).

The Main Event is a live album of highlights from a series of concerts in Madison Square Garden, New York. It showcases Sinatra's extraordinary range as a singer from exuberant up-tempo anthems to high living and wrenching ballads. It is widely judged to be the best release of his twilight years.

Trilogy is more portentous in conception and organization. As we have already noted, it consists of three albums covering Sinatra's *Past*, *Present* and *Future*. The most successfully realized is the *Past*, arranged and conducted by Billy May, which blazingly rekindles the romantic aura of the Swing Era. The last disc on *Trilogy* – *Future* – is widely held to be the low point of the set and the nadir of Sinatra's career. Arranged and conducted by Sinatra's old standby, Gordon Jenkins, the disc is a confused, undistinguished oration on space travel, world peace, and the wonders of nature.

She Shot Me Down is generally considered as a partial return to form. Most of the tracks are tastefully arranged and conducted, by Gordon Jenkins. Sinatra added five new songs to his repertoire, two standards and two "rediscovered" pieces. He seems hesitant with some of the new material, as if he is finding it harder to impress his stamp upon the songs. The verve that seemed natural in most of his recordings in the 1950s and 1960s seems here to be labored. Nonetheless, the album boasts classic recordings of *Thanks for the Memory*, the Nelson Riddle medley *The Gal That Got Away/It Never Entered My Mind*, and a surprisingly effective version of the Sonny Bono song *Bang Bang*.

His remaining work was compromised by a misplaced desire to appear "contemporary" by either recording new songs by the likes of Neil Diamond, Paul Anka, John Denver, Jimmy Webb, Kris Kristofferson, and Barry Manilow – apparently judged by Sinatra to be "hot" – or reworking standards from his back catalog. The last albums that Sinatra recorded, *Duets* (1993) and *Duets II* (1994) are in effect tribute albums in which he revisits standards from his repertoire with guest duettists. Among those involved were Barbara Streisand, Tony Bennett,

Aretha Franklin, Gloria Estefan, Lena Horne, Gladys Knight, Willie Nelson, Liza Minelli, Carly Simon, Patti Labelle, Luis Miguel, Jon Secada, Neil Diamond, Jimmy Buffet, Linda Ronstadt, Chrissie Hynde, Luther Vandross, and Bono. Many critics lambasted these recordings as a triumph of technology over art. This is because none of the tracks actually involve Sinatra duetting with his guests in the studio. The "duettists" recorded their contribution on different dates and phoned them in using a digital telephone line. The music was subsequently spliced together by sound engineers and the producer. Some tracks are resplendent. The reworkings of *One for My Baby, Embraceable You* and *Where or When?* are all notable additions to the Sinatra canon. But the general critical response was regret that Sinatra resorted to formula recordings at the end of his career rather than attempting something genuinely new. Several critics describe the recordings as hackneyed and deplore the projects as revenue-raising exercises. They were certainly commercially successful, especially *Duets*, and arguably opened the ears of younger generations to Sinatra's music. They did not add much polish to the Sinatra legend. However, they displayed showmanship and staying power.

Sinatra on Television

Interestingly, the one genre of popular entertainment in which Sinatra failed was television. He experimented with the medium early on. In 1950 he debuted as a guest on Bob Hope's TV special *The Star-Spangled Revue*. The performance was judged to be promising enough for CBS to launch a series of hour-long variety show specials, *The Frank Sinatra Show*, which began airing in the prime-time Saturday evening slot between 9 and 10 p.m., later in the same year. The critical response was lukewarm, although audience reactions were positive enough to persuade CBS to continue the series, albeit switching the broadcast to the lower profile slot of 9 p.m. on Tuesday nights. Sinatra's performances were stilted, perhaps a reflection of his continuing difficulties with Ava Gardner and the general desperation of his

"Dark Ages." He was most confident in vocal performances. His comedy banter either faltered or misfired.

There was a five-year gap between the first and the second series, punctuated with guest appearances on TV shows and specials. Sinatra returned in 1957 with a new version of *The Frank Sinatra Show*, broadcast this time between 9 and 10 on Friday evenings. In a typical display of bravado Sinatra claimed ultimate control over production and insinuated that others were to blame for the failure of the first series: "If I fall on my face, I want to be the cause... All of the years when I was taking advice from others they told me wrong 50 percent of the time" (Humphrey 1957: 13). But the second series was quickly dismissed as formulaic and unimaginative. ABC cancelled in 1958.

In contrast, many of Sinatra's one-off TV specials in the 1950s were lauded by the critics and relished by the public. His role as the singing stage manager in the 1955 version of Thornton Wilder's *Our Town* is regarded to be a classic performance. His *Edsel Show* appearance in 1957 with Bing Crosby amalgamated two generations of vocal styles as triumphantly as the Sinatra/ Crosby film *High Society* in 1956. Even Sinatra's performance with Elvis Presley in the 1960 *Welcome Home Elvis* show is remembered as a notable curio in which Sinatra confronted a rock'n'roll persona that he despised and earned a 45.1 trendex rating – the highest ever for a Sinatra show.

Yet Sinatra never emulated Dean Martin's durable TV success. Why was this? Albert Auster (1999) provides an interesting explanation of Sinatra's relative failure as a TV performer. Borrowing from the terminology of the media theorist Marshall McLuhan, he argues that Sinatra was a "hot"-medium performer ill-suited to the "cool" medium of the television variety show. A hot medium presupposes high definition data and audience familiarity with the medium, presenting obvious barriers for audience access. A cool medium is based on low definition data and minimal audience familiarity with the medium, thus maximizing audience access. Translating this into different words, Auster's point is that Sinatra's performing style relied too heavily on audience identification with the look, the stage persona, and his onstage intensity. More laid back performers like Bing Crosby, Perry Como and Dean Martin operated better in the television variety show format because their manner was more relaxed and easygoing. Auster notes that Sinatra tended to use in-jokes, double entendres and urbane Broadway witticisms as part of his television patter. These references either went over the heads of the audience or made them feel uninformed and stupid. What worked triumphantly onstage at the Copacabana Club became supercilious and smug when transferred to a television studio. Auster (1999: 171) approvingly quotes a review from *Variety* (December 26, 1957) which distils the main problem with *The Frank Sinatra Show:*

> The worst aspect of the show, and the facet that seems to cause most discomfort is dialogue, with Sinatra spouting a list of flip expressions that are supposed to be sophisticated and hip but come across as completely mannered...He can work all the tension he wants into a song or even a performance, but on television you've got to be relaxed and you've got to be straightforward and believable, or it's murder, as Sinatra is now experiencing.

After the Rat Pack

After the demise of the Rat Pack, the other member of Fort Sinatra experienced varying degrees of success. Dean Martin rivaled Sinatra's success after 1965, with hugely popular recordings like *Let It Snow, Let It Snow, Let It Snow* (1966), *Little Ole Wine Drinker Me* (1967), *By the Time I Get to Phoenix, Gentle on My Mind* (1968); and films like the popular Matt Helm series of camp spy films (*The Silencers*, 1966, *Murderer's Row*, 1966, *The Ambushers*, 1968, and *The Wrecking Crew*, 1969), and *Airport* (1970), one of only a dozen films made between 1950 and 1970 to make $45 million. However, his biggest success after 1965 was arguably the weekly *Dean Martin Show* for NBC Television which ran from September 1965 to April 1974. Pointedly, he excelled in a medium in which Sinatra spectacularly flopped. In these shows he established a new relationship with his core audience of middle America by emphasizing the ramshackle, couldn't-care-less features of his stage and recording personality. The values of the show were defiantly contrary to the diet of peace and love followed by the counterculture. As Tosches puts it:

> "The Dean Martin Show" was an immense and immediate success. His uncaring manner and good-natured boorishness endeared him to millions who were sick of sincerity, relevance, and pseudo-sophistication... In him, for one late hour before the final day of every workweek, the multitudes, tired and half-drunk and onward-slouching, found something of their own: lullaby and vindication, justification and inspiration, a bit of boozy song and a glimpse of gal-meat. (1992: 373)

Sammy Davis Jr also enjoyed continued success after the Rat Pack through television specials, films, recordings, and stage performances. But his career was blighted by the drug dependence that estranged him from Sinatra in the late 1960s and for most of the 1970s. He was always eclipsed by Sinatra and Martin and did not object to taking third billing on the ill-fated *Together Again* tour. Although the youngest of the Rat Pack, he died eight years almost to the day before Sinatra, on May 16, 1990.

Peter Lawford suffered the most tragic and precipitate decline. After breaking with Sinatra following the "Californian White House" debacle, he dabbled in nightclub performances as the straight man for Jimmy Durante. But his film and television work was slight and he succumbed to the effects of alcohol and drug addiction in 1984.

Joey Bishop became the most retiring member of the Rat Pack. In 1967 he tried to reinvent himself by fronting a late night talk show for ABC, but he was replaced after two years by Dick Cavett. His late career became ever more peripatetic, with appearances on talk shows and quiz shows, character parts in TV series, and the occasional movie. Golf, fishing and sailing seemed to occupy more and more of his time.

In a sense it was symbolic of the fate of all the Rat Pack. Bishop may not have enjoyed the commercial success of Sinatra, Martin or Davis Jr, but his post–Rat Pack career expressed more powerfully that their time had passed. Sinatra constructed the Rat Pack as a bastion of male cool which celebrated the accumulation of wealth, sexual license, endless leisurely rounds of golf, fooling around, and hedonism. Implicitly it was counterposed to both the straight values of middle America (which nonetheless comprised its core audience) and the Brahmin code of social superiority practiced by the elite. It drew a good deal of its artistic and ribald energy from antagonizing both of these sources. Yet when the doctrine of liberation and permissiveness it espoused extended to feminism, militant black power and the counterculture, it back-pedaled as a notably reactionary force in American popular culture. By the mid-1960s the Rat Pack was widely acknowledged to be a period piece – a ghastly eventuality for Sinatra, who always prided himself on his artistic and social relevance. But even he recognized that times change.

The Rat Pack remained a high-water mark in his career. Arguably, it was the time when he achieved the greatest continuous fulfillment as a performer. However, the attempt to revive the glory days in the *Together Again* and *Ultimate Event* tours of 1988 cruelly exposed the group as little more than a nostalgia act. Yet even then, Sinatra could not retire gracefully. He continued to perform, to record, to cajole others to do his bidding, to make grand social pronouncements, to position himself in places where he could exert influence, and to broker political deals of all kinds. His thirst for power and mass acclaim remained unslaked.

―――― five ――――

ENVOI

Sinatra regarded himself as being above all a saloon singer. The emphasis on demotic appeal is pronounced in his work. Although he was a harsh taskmaster on stage and in the recording studio, what comes through most powerfully in the recollections of those who worked with him was his musicianship and camaraderie. He liked singing with a band so that he could look everyone in the eye (Granata 1999). He was of the people, and his elevation in consumer culture depended upon ritually acknowledging his earthbound, urban-industrial origins on the wrong side of the tracks in Hoboken.

This "tough background" was deliberately exaggerated. Although he suffered racial abuse in youth, he sprang from relatively prosperous small-business/public service roots. He became an American Caesar in the entertainment industry, but his status is of a discordant achieved celebrity, implicitly and often openly opposed to ascribed authority, especially when it took the form of the privileges of the establishment. Sinatra's elevation to achieved celebrity dramatized migrant experience and symbolized upward mobility in a century that vastly multiplied the chances for Americans of acquiring nouveau riche status. For every luckless small-time gambler pulling one-armed bandits on the Las Vegas strip, and each parvenu success story taking residence in a mansion in the Hollywood Hills, Sinatra represented a sort of universal standard of achieved celebrity. If someone from his unprepossessing background could rise to the top, anyone could. Unapologetic about his achievements, true to his own contradictory moral code, redefining the notion of cool from black jazz culture and emblazing it in white popular culture, Sinatra between the 1940s and 1950s and arguably up to the mid-1960s provided nothing less than "the soundtrack of the age" (Witkin 2003: 176).

Sinatra was also, importantly, an addictive personality. This characteristic is common in the lives of achieved celebrities. It mirrors the addiction to the acquisitive values of consumer culture that permeates their fan base. It is important to emphasize the causal relationship between consumer culture and achieved celebrity. Achieved celebrities are the product of societies in which the psychology of wanting is constituted as a legitimate goal for the general population. The desire to be more than you are, to accumulate more than you possess, opposes ancient hierarchy and the obstacles of rank to make achievement a general cultural goal. Achievement goes hand-in-hand with accumulation, and both only become psychologically and culturally pronounced in mature consumer society. Sinatra drank too much, partied too long, and persisted touring despite being in failing health. He was also tenacious, demonstrating both a ruthless streak to maintain and develop his position in popular entertainment and a marked reluctance to leave the public stage. Again, this is common in the lives of achieved celebrities. What accounts for it?

Achieved celebrities often rationalize their tenacious dependence on public life in pious terms, by insisting that they need to earn money to maintain their lifestyles and support their families. The nub of this argument is that celebrity life is expensive. To be taken seriously by fans, dedicated flamboyance and conspicuous consumption are *de rigueur*. There is some truth in this position. Achieved celebrities need to lead their lives in technicolor so as to contrast with the monochrome hues of their fan base, and through this means to offer a conspicuous standard of emulation and fantasy.

But the strength of the argument is diminished by the complaints made by achieved celebrities that their public success destroys their private life. The engulfment of the private self is a condition that threatens the achieved celebrity. This was certainly true of Sinatra. He resented media intrusion into his private life and was often dismissive of fans who sought to share his own time. Yet he found it almost impossible to retire and only did so when his health became a public issue.

A more plausible motive for the tenacity of achieved celebrity is that it is psychologically seductive, permitting recipients of this status to live with *élan,* mobility and, if they elect, thin emotional and moral responsibilities. We know that achieved celebrities have a higher general propensity to divorce and be promiscuous (Fowles 1992) than ordinary people. We know that most dread descent and the fall from public attention (Rojek 2001). The quest for *distinction,* either as a way of maximizing sexual conquests or of possessing an automatic and unequivocally enviable status in society, is then a credible motive behind achieved celebrity. Interestingly, the prime drive behind achieved celebrity on this account is not, strictly speaking, the pursuit of self-satisfaction, but the acquisition of distinction *in the sight of others.* It is the adulation and honor that others invest in the celebrity that is the crux of achieved celebrity status.

Yet if that is the case, it does not explain why our interest in achieved celebrities is so morally indiscreet. After all, we know that we are fascinated by the amorality and violence of achieved celebrities just as much as by their integrity and goodness. Consider: if the world of achieved celebrity consisted of infinite replicas of Mother Teresa, it would almost certainly cease to occupy a pivotal position in culture. Most of us soon tire of a diet of unvarying integrity and goodness and possess a prurient interest in exploring the dark side of distinction. Famously, Christopher Hitchens (1995) even sought to debunk Mother Teresa with an expose of her relations with right-wing dictators and tycoons.[1]

The grip that Sinatra exerted in popular culture for six decades cogently reflected public fascination with the amoral, bellicose side of his personality. Public interest in the dark side of achieved celebrity seems to be a corollary of the fascination with legitimate success. An entire genre of celebrity exposure exists through the media of gossip columns, tabloid journalism, and investigative television. Its purpose is to find cracks in the facade of achieved celebrity. While it is routinely condemned in public life, with phrases like "checkbook or muckraking journalism" often used, it is immensely popular, bankrolling publications like The *National Inquirer, Heat,* and *Closer.* Since there is a constant demand for this material in Western culture the conclusion must be that the public needs idols, but fantasizes about them having feet of clay.

The Religion of Achieved Celebrity

What then, over and above the rise of *gesellschaft* relations and the fragmentation, mobility and discontinuity associated with them, accounts for the centrality of achieved celebrity in Western culture today? The decline of organized religion is crucial. Of course, people retain religious and spiritual feelings, but they are less often organized in the form of beliefs in the teachings of a particular church. If the need for feelings of elevation and gravity are no longer supplied by a belief in God, might they be fulfilled by devotion to secular achieved celebrities? Sinatra was a religious man, but his piety and strong sense of irreverence would have caused him to recoil from the notion that he was regarded by some as a secular god. But might this be the way in which he was actually widely viewed in popular culture as early as the bobbysoxer hysteria of the early 1940s?

Unquestionably, a series of illuminating parallels can be drawn between religious belief systems and achieved celebrity cultures. Both operate with the distinction between the profane world of everyday existence, and the sacred world embodied by the object of devotion or achieved celebrity; each has developed an elaborate set of rituals in religious and celebrity worship; each is based in the principle that worship is a mark of social inclusion which separates the devotee from the profane world; and in religious culture, and celebrity culture, systems of preserving and exchanging relics have developed which invest the object of devotion with the gloss of immortality. Arguably, in secularized society, the lives of achieved celebrities are ubiquitous through media representations, while the presence of religious figures is not.

If all of this is the case, might these lives offer *parables* for conduct that were once supplied by organized religion? In following the elevation and descent of achieved celebrities might we be primarily motivated by the urge to learn larger lessons or rules for our own behavior? It goes without saying that these parables are not always edifying. The psychological travails and highly public deaths of Marilyn Monroe, Montgomery Clift, Marvin Gaye, Kurt Cobain and River Phoenix, to name but a few, illustrate the morbidity of fame. A parable is a story that helps people find moral orientation in the world. Its content can be good or bad. In following the life story of Michael Jackson, Madonna, Michael Jordan, O. J. Simpson, Gary Glitter, Tom Cruise, Stephen Spielberg, Michael Caine or Jennifer Lopez, we gain life-scripts and see parallels that we apply to everyday life. I submit that in secular societies organized around systems of mass communication, celebrity parables have emerged as part of the conditioning process for popular behavior.

It might be objected that this line of reasoning, which identifies achieved celebrity as a substitute for organized religious belief, fails to get to grip with the commercialization of celebrity cultures. On this account, the public interest in the likes of achieved celebrities is a consequence of the commodification of celebrity culture. This in turn identifies the corporation as the key agent behind the exalted status of achieved celebrity in contemporary culture. So much so that corporations are said to have the capacity to improvise celebrity by organizing what Boorstin (1960) called "pseudo-events" or creating "celetoids."

The commercialization of achieved celebrity is so pronounced in our culture that the argument is powerful and may even appear to be self-evident. But this ignores two things. First, organized religion is also heavily commercialized and commodified, and has been at least since the time of the medieval pilgrimages.[2] Second, commercialization and commodification are symptoms of our profound need for symbols of continuity, elevation, and gravity. In secularized society, in the absence of organized religion to satisfy this need, the culture of commercialized, commodified achieved celebrity is left to fill the breech.

Sinatra and the Parables of Achieved Celebrity

Perhaps then, another way of reading Sinatra and achieved celebrities in general is to regard them as *envois* communicating compelling parables – about the struggles of masculinity and femininity, aspiration and fulfillment, romance, work and play, dignity and failure – to the masses from the position of those who have ascended so meteorically from their midst. Celebrities personalize and hence make accessible the contradictions between the central myths of achievement culture and common experience. Achievement culture presents personal success as the universal goal of social membership. At the same time it perpetuates economic inequality and distributes the personal chances of attaining success unequally. Celebrities provide parallels of success and failure in the lives of the unsuccessful. They offer a basis for identification and recognition for both the ambitious and the lonely, and so allow the conflicts generated by thwarted experiences in work, romance and family life to be reconciled.

In effect, one function of achieved celebrity culture is to provide scripts for life management. The lives of celebrities operate as parables that are applied in everyday life to generate aspirational or cautionary examples and to fill a vacuum caused by the decline of religion and achievement famine in the lives of fans. This is to emphasize the integrative functions of celebrity culture and to do so is appropriate in conditions where tenable moral frameworks associated with organized religion are in disarray. However, celebrities can also function as the bearers of a critical consciousness that challenges convention. They are agents of change as well as cultural reproduction.

Sinatra played both roles throughout his career. His fabulous, legendary acts of generosity, the glorification of the nice 'n' easy lifestyle in Palm Springs and Nevada, were in hindsight consistently vulgar. They exposed the depth of his need to flaunt wealth and achievements through conspicuous consumption, and also the public desire to be reminded of his success. Inasmuch as they dramatized the acquisitive logic of consumer culture, they were integrative in that they provided aspirational life-scripts that operated to reproduce the central values of the system. Conversely, his spendthrift attitude disguised a tenacious work ethic in musical recording, film, television and concert performance that far outstripped that of most of his contemporaries. Some of his habitual excesses in violence, hard drinking and sexual relations may reflect the demanding work schedule he set himself, especially after the Dark Ages, when for nearly six years he peered into the abyss of celebrity descent. Sinatra's life mirrored his dichotomous, Manichean moral system. He sought extravagant rewards as recompense for his toils.

However, the exaggerated display of pleasure in consumption is also the classic hallmark of the uneducated parvenu who comes from nowhere and is determined to leave his imprimatur upon all levels of the world through display and an apparent indifference to money. In his youth and middle age, Sinatra could never simply relax. He had to relax *more* than other people, with greater verve, exhibition, and enjoyment. Paradoxically this involved greater *effort*. The competitive streak that dominated his recording, film and concert work carried over into his partying, drinking, parenting, and sexual relationships. His driven character was widely commented upon by his family, friends, and contemporaries. Sinatra's riches were not the result of inheritance, they were earned by the sweat of his brow. His achievements were a monument to the work ethic. Inasmuch as this is true, his career reinforced the moral maxim that hard work brings reward and enhances the system.

Yet in at least three respects, Sinatra also offered a more challenging, controversial role model. First, he was one of the first achieved celebrities in the entertainment industry to be *insouciant* about his political involvement and convictions. In the 1940s and 1950s his identification with the left and the civil rights movement taunted middle America and stereotyped him as a figure of controversy. His insouciance revealed a new disposition among popular entertainers that challenged the authority of production companies and gossip columnists. Sinatra humanized celebrity culture by defiantly insisting on a warts-and-all approach to the media and public.

167

Second, FBI files demonstrate that he maintained connections with the Mafia despite public disquiet and highly embarrassing public investigations. Somewhat lamely, Sinatra claimed that his sole involvement with notorious Mafia ringleaders and their henchmen was the friendship ties that follow his type of Italian-American background. As we have seen, Tina Sinatra (2000) makes the same argument in her memoir of her father. Sinatra seems to have relished his public association with organized crime. Perhaps it appealed to his machismo. He'd grown up in an Italian community enthralled by the Castellammarese wars and the tough-guy films of Edward G. Robinson, James Cagney, Paul Muni, and George Raft in the 1930s. It also identified him as a genuine tough guy in Hollywood, which arguably enhanced his substance as a businessman and certainly distinguished him from other celebrities who merely adopted the role of tough guy on screen.

Third, artistically and in business terms, Sinatra was arguably the first renegade artist in mass popular entertainment of the electronic era. He abandoned the Tommy Dorsey Band in 1942 to pursue a solo career. At the time this was an extremely risky venture. There was no guarantee that Sinatra would be accepted as a solo singer. The precedents of lead vocalists who had gone on to achieve solo success were not auspicious. Among Sinatra's own generation, Bob Eberly, Dick Haymes and Jack Leonard had tried to go it alone and failed. His break with Columbia Records in 1952 followed an acrimonious debate with Mitch Miller, A&R Director of the company, on the question of artistic control. Almost a decade later he parted from Capitol Records after the company refused to meet his demands for creative control and an improved financial package. Sinatra established the precedent for major artists to take on record companies and manage their own business affairs. He founded his own record company, Reprise Records, in 1961 and demonstrated that artists could take artistic and business control of their own affairs. He contributed to an ethos of independence in celebrity culture and virtually pioneered the tradition of the popular vocalist as *auteur*.

The Urban-Industrial Legato

The urban-industrial context of Sinatra's art is crucial. He relished readymade eloquence and the use of the vernacular. His best work has a poetic quality that perfectly encapsulates the contrariness, dislocation, estrangement and isolation of the individual in mass consumer culture. He conveys a romantic conviction that individual emotions can rise above the mechanization and standardization of the corporate-state imposed environment.

Sinatra's habitat is the city. His audience is the masses caught up in the emotional, physical, economic and cultural perturbation of the urban juggernaut. The braggadocio he employs in songs like *The Lady Is a Tramp*, *It Was a Very Good Year* and *My Way*, answers to the popular mass experience of unrequited love, economic uncertainty, personal insignificance, and the inexorable, disappearance of youth. Even in romantic numbers like *All the Way*, *I'll Never Smile Again* and *Embraceable You* there is a hint of impending menace. The songs seem to ponder the decay of relationships even as they celebrate their birth. His work encapsulates the evanescence and fugitive nature of human relationships. After the final split with Ava Gardner, Sinatra's phrasing is of a man who expects to be let down in love. The song that he partly composed about his relationship with Ava, *I'm a Fool to Want You*, aches with incredulity about the strength of his abiding desire for her, despite her repeated infidelity. Yet it also clearly expresses his helplessness as he is drawn again like a moth to a flame.

Sinatra's romantic legato style is crammed with references to being wounded and let down. Women are idealized in most of his songs as objects of desire. He celebrates their grace, wit, and companionship. But they are also sometimes presented as shrewish, ungrateful, and finally untrustworthy. Yet he constantly returns to the role of a hopeless romantic, forever believing that fidelity is "a sacred trust" (Kempton 1998: 13).

Sinatra and the Problem of Acquiescence in Popular Culture

This raises the question of how much this was merely a *role* for Sinatra. The association between singing and acting was always strong in his mind. As he told *Playboy* in 1963: "You begin to learn to use the lyrics of a song as a script, as a scene. I didn't know I was doing that at the time, but I was" (quoted in Lahr 1998: 30). This suggests a degree of artfulness and calculation in Sinatra's work from which the inference might be made that he was both detached from the emotions he conveyed and consciously manipulated the audience. But it is also how many listeners hear popular music. Perhaps one should recall at this point the many hours that Sinatra spent in the 1920s and 1930s listening to the new medium of coast-to-coast radio. He was imaginatively projecting himself into other situations, playing roles and fantasizing about articulating the emotions of strangers. If one reads Sinatra from the standpoint of critical theory, the suggestions of calculation and manipulation quickly become accentuated.

For example, Robert Witkin (2003: 171–2), in a homage to Adorno which takes the form of a "thought experiment" in the manner of the master's style, highlights the *performative* character of Sinatra's work and uses it to make a wider case that popular entertainment colludes with alienation. For Witkin, again adopting the "voice" of Adorno:

> A good vocalist with good phrasing – and Sinatra has that – will be able to produce "soulfulness" and sincerity for you – as you would expect of a fine actor. That does not make the sentiments expressed true. I have always believed that feelings expressed in this sensuous way, in modern works of art, are a form of consolation, of acquiescence and of false consciousness, through which the subject affects reconciliation to the world and its condition of social dependency. The subject who weeps for consolation in this vale of tears has no resistance to offer, can do nothing to ready the spirit to summon better times. (2003: 172)

This reading is consistent with Adorno's philosophy, but it undervalues the *instructive* element in Sinatra's best work. Sinatra claimed that he followed the Italian bel canto style of lyrical operatic singing which attempts a rich broad tone and smooth phrasing (Granata 1999: 12). Bel canto singing makes a virtue of concise, heartfelt, noncircumlocutory delivery. Its staple themes are love and villainy and it uses the vernacular to maximize audience access. Love is presented as the highest happiness and source of noble inspiration.

All of these features are evident in Sinatra's choice of material and style of vocal delivery. His development of bel canto, legato style was a way of both encapsulating the density and textures of urban-industrial experience and making them pellucid. If the tumult of urban-industrial existence makes our experience of life amorphous and shapeless, Sinatra's songs provide a sense of intense, elevated focus. His music and films constantly give the impression that he has lived *more* than you. He has been more wounded, more thrilled, more weary, more entranced. Sinatra's music admitted vulnerability but it also seemed more worldly and knowledgeable than the experience of his audience. Occasionally, this was overbearing. But the association between Sinatra's music and intimacy occurs with too much frequency in the literature on audience responses to his work to dismiss (Petkov and Mustazza 1995; Hamill 1998). Sinatra's recordings and concerts unquestionably touched people and left the audience with the impression that the emotions he articulated were directly relevant to him.

If the art and behavior of achieved celebrities offer parables for the masses, Sinatra's music provided a sort of lifelong education class for mass urban-industrial people caught up in disjointed relations, unrequited love, glancing liaisons, moral confusion, vaulting ambition, and cloacal loneliness. It may not have produced a viable political alternative, but it expressed emotions and experiences that were *shared*.

Sinatra sings to the lonely, the slighted, the wanting and the needy, and in doing so he articulates an acquisitive, questing humanity that is the brand-mark of consumer culture. His personal life, which after his first success in the early 1940s was always public property, fixed him in the public mind as a man who fought, won and lost, and fought again. He is a far more combative vocalist than Bing Crosby, Al Jolson, Perry Como, or Dean Martin. His celebrity profile bridled at being stereotyped. This is one reason why he always raged against media attempts to pigeonhole him by age. Sinatra regarded himself to be above age and insisted that his art was universally relevant. It is easy to dwell on the narcissistic and autocratic overtones of this self-image. Arguably, to do so at length offers a distorted picture. Sinatra was unquestionably a narcissist and he could, on occasion, be autocratic. His presumption that he constituted an indisputable object of mass attention carried with it sullen forbearance in the face of the inquisitorial eye of the media and the public. His style of celebrity seldom spared him from admitting faults in his personality and predisposed him to ridicule other entertainers who behaved as if their careers circumnavigated an endless virtuous circle. Sinatra valued candor and honesty. His career contributed to the informalization of achieved celebrity culture inasmuch as he paved the way for, in his case, carefully edited disclosure and the cultivation of an unapologetic, rebarbative celebrity attitude to the media.

This is not to discount the Witkin–Adorno line of critical analysis. Sinatra was an arch manipulator of popular sentiment. But he always regarded himself as more *representative* of the conflicting emotions that typified his audience than, perhaps, the Witkin–Adorno line allows. As he told *Playboy* in 1963:

> I get an audience involved, personally involved in a song – because I'm involved myself... Being an eighteen carat manic-depressive and having lived a life of violent emotional contradictions, I have an overacute capacity for sadness as well as elation... Whatever else has been said about me personally is unimportant. When I sing, I believe I'm honest... You can be the most artistically perfect performer in the world, but an audience is like a broad – if you're indifferent, endsville. (Quoted in Shaw 1968: 317)

The observation that he possessed an "overacute capacity" for sadness and elation rings true. Perhaps the origins of this capacity are bio-chemical. I prefer to stress Sinatra's status as an only child and his addiction to the new forms of popular entertainment, radio and movies, in the 1920s and 1930s, which intensified his propensity to identify with others and imagine ways of articulating *their* fugitive emotions.

His best work makes a virtue of educating the public. The classic albums, *In the Wee Small Hours, Where Are You?, Only the Lonely,* and *No One Cares,* are attempts to encapsulate the spirit of abandonment, rejection, expansive desire and isolation that are the hallmarks of the modern urban-industrial experience. In them Sinatra is an *auteur* using his own well-publicized experience in life and love to produce art that illuminates the experience of the masses. Similarly, his greatest films, which in my view are *Suddenly, The Man with the Golden Arm, The Joker Is Wild,* and *The Manchurian Candidate,* challenge both the middle-brow orthodoxy and hypocrisy of middle America and the Brahmin complacency of the power elite. These were risky films for a pop idol to make and Sinatra should be given credit for trying to instruct popular opinion rather than pander to it.

If modern life propagates neurosis because it fastens on the dangers and worries of urban-industrial existence, it also encourages revenge. Sinatra's best work is romantic and assured, but it carries the parvenu's anxiety that success might be taken away at a stroke and emphasizes the value of persistent "high hopes." In numbers like *That's Life* (1966) and *Bad, Bad Leroy Brown* (1974) Sinatra presents urban-industrial existence as a wretched dog-fight. Will Friedwald rightly describes the former as "at once invigorating and a little disturbing" (1996: 197). In this material, Sinatra's pugilism is pronounced. The romantic lilt of Sinatra's version of *The Girl from Ipanema* (1967) is swept aside by the latent aggression of these recordings. In this Sinatra again articulates the common character of urban-industrial, market experience. Of course, he dramatizes and manipulates emotions since this is essential to the art of the best popular entertainers. Yet it does not follow that the emotions he conveys are therefore false and inauthentic. For audiences deprived of a public stage, Sinatra's voice offers resonance. Far from contributing to popular acquiescence, he articulates a basis for *identification* and *recognition*. Identification and recognition, I submit, are the basis for developing collective consciousness. Inasmuch as Sinatra presented his own experience and art as the *typification* of modern times it produced the political consequence of eliciting recognition of collectivism in the midst of general alienation. Yet he was never able to transcend contradiction by developing a coherent moral framework worthy of the genuine *uomo di rispetto*. He articulated contradiction, but failed to reconcile it. Nowhere more so than in his politics and attitude to masculinity.

Sinatra and the Quest for Power

Sinatra was interested in power. Admittedly, throughout his career his declared political affiliations changed radically. In the 1940s his identification with the left was bombastic and defiant. Sinatra was well aware that he nettled conservative opinion, but he cared not a jot. Equally, he knew that his allegiance to the Republican cause during the Reagan years incensed his liberal allies. After all, for most of the 1950s and early 1960s, Sinatra regarded Reagan as a reactionary buffoon. He would have known of Reagan's testimony as a "friendly witness" to the House of Un-American Activities Committee, and his enthusiastic role in cooperating with the blacklisting of actors, writers and directors suspected of having Communist sympathies. This undoubtedly soured his view of Reagan, whose move to the right in the 1950s was anathema to the left-leaning Sinatra. For the Holmby Hills Rat Pack, and later for Sinatra's own Rat Pack, Reagan was an unimaginative apologist for conservative values. Privately, Sinatra ridiculed Reagan's ambitions for a larger role on the political stage in the late 1950s and early 1960s. Publicly, he derided Reagan's campaign, as a Republican, to be Governor of California, and vilified his election victory in 1966.

However, when Reagan campaigned for reelection in 1970, Sinatra astounded and embarrassed many of his liberal and Democrat associates by pledging support for the Republican cause (Levy 1998: 298). He was a prominent and effective fundraiser and cheerleader for Reagan's presidential campaign.

He was a regular guest at the Reagan White House, and throughout the Clinton years he remained a staunch Republican.

What were the causes of this volte-face? Three points are relevant. First, Sinatra was mortified by John F. Kennedy's decision in 1962 to adopt the Republican Bing Crosby's Palm Springs home as the "Californian White House" in preference to Rancho Mirage. In his own mind Sinatra had been a kingmaker in Kennedy's presidential campaign. He felt rebuffed by Robert Kennedy's advice that Sinatra's involvement with the Mafia was too politically sensitive to risk arousing public suspicions of a grace and favor relationship between Sinatra and John F. Kennedy. Worse, he felt that a blood bond had been broken. As he expressed it to Angie Dickinson: "If he would only pick up the telephone and call me and say that it was politically difficult to have me around, I would understand. I don't want to hurt him. But he has never called me" (Schlesinger 1978: 496).

In a sense, politically speaking, Sinatra never recovered from this. If, before 1962, he felt that he was living in a fallen world, at least he had the pleasure of knowing that he assisted John F. Kennedy in adding glamour and excitement to public life. After Kennedy's rejection, Sinatra grew bitter, cynical, and more pragmatic. He now believed that the fundamentals of the world – competition, inequality and individualism – could not be changed by humanism or rational planning. Again, the punitive element in his character came to the fore. A key turning point appears to have been the 1972 Select Committee on Crime enquiry into his relations with the Mafia. The Californian Democratic Senator, John Tunney, led the Committee. Sinatra had known Tunney for many years. He even performed at a special fundraising concert for him which produced donations of $160,000. The Senator's involvement in leading an official Congressional committee into his private affairs struck Sinatra as akin to personal treachery.

Reagan's presidential campaign suggested a renewal of glamour and, more importantly, personal welcome to Sinatra after the grey years of Johnson, Nixon, Ford, and Carter. In an op-ed piece in the *New York Times*, published in 1972, Sinatra rationalized his turn to the right as the *continuation* of his lifelong beliefs.

He was still in favor of standing up for "the little guy." The difference was that now he regarded big government as the main threat to ordinary people. Sinatra was not alone in embracing Reagan's right-wing populism as the redefinition of American individualism. Initially at least, the Reagan Republicans tried to keep a public distance from Sinatra's involvement with the Reagan presidency. For example, after extensive fundraising, performing and organizing Reagan's inaugural gala, Sinatra was belittled by the Reagans in a highly public fashion. In the words of Quirk and Schoell.

> When it came to time for the inauguration itself...Sinatra discovered that he was not to be one of the chosen One Hundred allowed to stand on the steps of U.S. Capitol as the President was sworn in. Sinatra did not bother flying into a public rage – instead he simply marched up the steps and joined the One Hundred whether they liked it or not. (1998: 330)

Second, in the mid-1960s Sinatra was persuaded that a long-term campaign combining charity work and political networking was the best strategy to regain his gambling license. The decision by the Nevada Gaming Control Board to deprive him of his license in 1963 had confirmed Sinatra's belief that there was establishment prejudice against him. For him, it was a matter of personal injustice and public insult. He was determined to reverse the ruling and correctly decided that assisting Reagan in his campaign for the White House would create a useful precedent for cashing in future favors.

Third, by the end of the 1960s, like many of his generation, Sinatra was convinced that the permissive society had gone too far. For his critics, this was an irony to be savored. Had not Sinatra in the 1940s and 1950s created the precedent in Hollywood for the outspoken political rough diamond? Was his sexual behavior as an adored and spoiled pop star and his public freedom with alcohol not the template for celebrity excess in the 1960s and 1970s? Did he not offer consumer culture a model of masculine upward mobility and free thinking? In this sense Hollywood "radicals" like Jane Fonda, Robert Redford and Paul Newman, and self-destructive rock idols like Lenny Bruce, Jim Morrison, Janice Joplin, Frank Zappa, Dennis Hopper and Jimi Hendrix, were Sinatra's children. Be that as it may, by the late 1960s he had disowned any connection with them and the values they articulated, and had rejected what he regarded as their louche lifestyle.

What of Sinatra's attitude to masculinity? If one considers the prominence given to the ideal of the *uomo di rispetto* and *uomo d'onore* in traditional Sicilian culture a good deal of Sinatra's masculine contrariness is explained. Arguably, the Sicilian values of masculine decisiveness, clientism and patronage were inflated in Italian-American culture between the 1890s and 1950s, as a means of accomplishing distinction and social integration on foreign soil. From this culture Sinatra learned to appreciate the value of fugitive, secretive dealing, and of displays of generosity, and the wisdom of creating the appearance of honesty and cultivating links with men and women of influence. His own personality contained a strong streak of belligerence, with repeated recourse to intimidation and physical violence, and association with known criminals such as Willie Moretti, Joe Fischetti, Sam Giancana, and Carlo Gambino. He could be intensely protective of those loyal to him – his tribe. Equally, he took seriously the Old Testament proverb, "If thine eye offend thee pluck it out." His behavior toward perceived malefactors like Peter Lawford, Joey Bishop, and on two occasions, Sammy Davis Jr, was malicious and vindictive.

Sinatra was capable of great friendship, but his code of masculinity was judgmental and punitive. This carried over into his relations with women. His narcissism advanced the ultimate ascendance of his own inscrutable interests and needs. His insensitive treatment of Lauren Bacall and Juliet Prowse was gratuitous. Faced with a personal or moral dilemma that he found insoluble and therefore distressing, Sinatra typically chose abandonment and rejection over compromise and conciliation.

The quest for power is the dominant motif in Sinatra's masculinity and career. I have interpreted it as driven by the need to be accepted as an equal at the table of the American power elite. At the same time his attitude to the power elite was deeply ambivalent. He held the common view of the upwardly mobile, that the establishment was decadent, vain, inefficient, and indifferent to the accomplishments and conditions of "the little guy." Yet he valued the elite's status and influence.

That he was ambitious and occasionally amoral in his quest for establishment acceptance is demonstrated by the extraordinary revelation in Tina Sinatra's memoir that Sinatra worked for many years for the CIA. As she put it:

> Whenever I wanted to reach him, no matter where he had flown, I had simply to call the White House switchboard, identify myself and ask them to find my dad for me. Within moments he'd be on the line. I tried it several times, and it worked like a charm.
>
> Years later, Dad confided why the White House tracked his whereabouts: he served as a courier for the CIA and the State Department, a not uncommon practice for citizens with private planes and the ability to slip in and out of places. Sometimes he carried papers, other times people. "It's no big deal," Dad told me. "I'm never in any danger. But you cannot tell anybody about it."
> (2000: 143)

In this passage Tina Sinatra contends that it was "not uncommon" for citizens with private planes to carry papers, and at other times people, for the CIA. Perhaps, but it was also hugely inconsistent with Sinatra's condemnation of the Hollywood witch-hunt and HUAC hearings of the 1940s, and his participation in these years with the Joint Anti-Fascist Committee and the Free Italy Society. It is important to note here that the CIA is not merely a patriotic organization. It is dedicated to covertly exploiting and developing American state-corporate interests worldwide. A clandestine role in its operations probably appealed strongly to Sinatra's sense of self-importance. This may partly account for the grating military bearing he often assumed after the end of the "Dark Ages." By working for the CIA Sinatra joined a cable of influence to the American power elite that functioned to achieve the covert manipulation of public opinion and the furtherance of global American corporate-state interests. Although most of the FBI files relating to Sinatra have been declassified, his work with the CIA remains confidential and is unlikely to be disclosed to the public. It cannot be stated with confidence that Sinatra was directly involved in the repression of critical and dissident voices. Conversely, he was employed by an organization committed to these ends as part of a project to enhance American global corporate-state influence.

"Those princes," wrote Machiavelli, "who adapt their conduct to circumstances are rarely unfortunate. Fortune is only changeable to those who cannot conform to the varying exigencies of the times; for we see different men take different courses to obtain the end they have in view" (1898: 482). Sinatra knew the value of changing his behavior according to "the exigencies of the times." His career in popular entertainment was one of the great passion plays of the modern entertainment industry. Latent menace vied with warmth and generosity in his personality. There were perpetual threatening undercurrents in his public gestures and private friendships. He regularly used dissemblance and intrigue to enhance his standing in the entertainment industry. Paradoxically, this fatally compromised his desire to be accepted as a man of honor and respect. When the public witnessed his charity work and oleaginous statements on behalf of the "little guy," many suspected that the mask of a dove hid the face of a cobra.

Sinatra could be perverse, truculent, and sadistic. This unbalanced the public perception of his genuine impulses toward generosity and humanity. His career is one of the best expressions of the psychology and politics of achieved celebrity in the twentieth century. Let his epitaph be the *bon mot* he is said to have uttered upon reaching the age of 50: "You only live once – and the way I live, once is enough."

179

NOTES

1 Frank's World

1 Of course I am aware of taking a liberty here. America entered the war in 1917, two years after Sinatra's birth. But I think it is worth retaining the description of him as a World War One baby for two reasons. First, it accords with Sinatra's apparently intrinsic sense of personal drama and significance. Although he was capable of great acts of kindness and thoughtfulness, Sinatra always regarded himself to be a charismatic presence, a *uomo di rispetto*. Second, he was the first and only child of migrants for whom the conflict in Europe must have seemed close to home well before Woodrow Wilson persuaded the Senate and Congress to vote to enter the war in April of 1917.

2 Mortimer had Sinatra arrested and charged with assault and battery. The suit was settled by an out of court payment made by Sinatra the day before trial was due to commence.

3 In fact Sinatra refused to bark. Although Sinatra sang with Dagmar, Miller was required to hire another performer to play the part of the dog.

4 Only one year before, in 1945, the same body had authorized him to receive the Outstanding Achievement Award for "industry relations."

5 Levy (1998: 214) notes that Sinatra got the dates wrong. Kennedy's only overnight stay at the estate was in November of 1959.

6 Sun City was actually located in Bophuthatswana, a "black homeland" client state set up by the South African government to gain international sympathy. Bophuthatswana was a public relations fiasco and it failed to gain recognition from any significant state in the international community.

2 *Uomo di Rispetto*

1 Dolly bestowed an ambiguous attitude to officialdom upon Frank. From her, he gained the prejudice that the American estabishment is introspective and vain. Conversely, she taught him that flattering the establishment and rewarding them with "favors" increased influence in the community.

2 In Australia the 59-year-old Sinatra abused the press corps, calling the men "a bunch of fags" and the women "hookers." He refused to withdraw his remarks, which resulted in him being blacklisted by the Stagehands Union and the Waiters Union. The Transport Union refused to refuel his jet, thus preventing him from returning to the US. Eventually, he issued a joint statement with the Australian Labor Union which gave him egress, but he never apologized.

3 Sinatra equated physical toughness with cultural preeminence. This was an old-fashioned, well nigh preindustrial view which probably owed much to the folk values of Sicily that he was exposed to in Hoboken.

4 Stompanato was eventually the victim of one of Hollywood's most infamous murders. He entered into a relationship with the Hollywood screen idol Lana Turner. In an argument at Turner's house on April 4, 1958, Stompanato was fatally stabbed by Turner's 14-year-old daughter.

3 Antinomies of Achieved Celebrity

1 Wills (1997: 107–13) portrays Wayne as a dedicated absenteeist from the war, who aimed to capitalize on the public impact he had achieved in the John Ford directed movie *Stagecoach*, made in 1939 as war broke out in Europe, to seal his stardom.

2 Clinton was attending a Group of Eight summit in Birmingham, UK, when Sinatra died. He released a written statement which reveals the Olympian position that Sinatra had attained in American popular entertainment by the time of his death. The full text reads:

> Hillary and I were deeply saddened to hear of the death of a musical legend and an American icon, Frank Sinatra. Early in his long career, fans dubbed him "The Voice". And that was the first thing America noted about Frank Sinatra: that miraculous voice, strong and subtle, wisecracking and wistful,

streetwise but defiantly sweet. In time he became so much more. Sinatra was a spellbinding performer, on stage and on screen, in musicals, comedies and dramas. He built one of the world's most important record companies. He won countless awards, from the Grammy – nine times – to the Academy Award, to the Presidential Medal of Freedom. And he dedicated himself to humanitarian causes. When I became President, I had never met Frank Sinatra, although I was an enormous admirer of his. I had the opportunity after I became President to get to know him a little, to have dinner with him, to appreciate on a personal level what fans around the world, including me, appreciated from afar.

Frank Sinatra will be profoundly missed by millions around the world. But his music and movies will ensure that "Ol' Blue Eyes" is never forgotten. Today, I think every American would have to smile and say he really did it his way. Hillary and I would like to offer our condolences to Frank's wife, Barbara, and to his children, Nancy, Frank Jr and Tina. Our hearts are with them today. (www.cnn.com/ALLPOLITICS/1998/05/15/clinton.sinatra)

3   Jimmy Van Heusen's real name was Chester Babcock.

4   The Rat Pack

1   Bogart's family embodied respectable upper middle-class New York values. His father was a doctor and owned a townhouse at 245, West 103rd Street. The family appeared in a list of 20,000 "fashionable homes" in *Dau's New York Blue Book*. The Bogarts owned a 55-acre summer estate on the shoreline of Canandaigua Lake, West New York state. Bogart's background could not have been more at odds with that of the low life outsiders he played on stage and screen

2   The war developed in two phases. Between 1946 and 1954 the Communist-led Nationalists, the Viet Minh, struggled for independence from French colonial rule. This ended in 1954 when two independent states were created, Communist North Vietnam and non-Communist South Vietnam. The second phase (1955–75) involved the struggle of North and South Vietnamese Communists (the Viet Cong) to seize power in South Vietnam and reunite the country. It was in this second phase that the US became militarily embroiled in the conflict. In 1955 President Eisenhower committed

the US to defend the territorial integrity of South Vietnam. American military advisors were despatched to the region to train South Vietnamese troops. By 1960 there were 900 advisors in the country. In 1961, in response to the increasing military threat posed by the Viet Cong, President Kennedy attached 400 Special Forces troops to engage in covert operations in Laos and Cambodia. He also increased the number of US troops stationed in the region to 16,300. US involvement increased dramatically after Kennedy's assassination. Under Johnson and Nixon the offensive escalated, with the US Air Force carrying out 526,000 bombing missions, and by 1969, 536,000 US troops were serving in the region. Altogether, 47,000 US servicemen were killed in the conflict.

3   Reprise was founded on the philanthropic principle that all rights would revert to the artist after a specified period – hence the title of the company. In 1963 Sinatra sold the company to Warner Brothers for $3 million and immediately reinvested $2 million for one-third ownership of the new Warner Brothers-Reprise label.

4   Sinatra's train collection consisted of 250 model trains on an 18 by 30 foot layout of stations and track. The layout replicated the Lionel train showroom setup that Sinatra visited as a young boy in New York. The train stations included his old neighborhood in Hoboken, a Wild West town, and a New Orleans riverboat. One train was decorated with his initials in diamonds and he had a crystal replica of the 1025 Chattanooga Choo Choo.

5   Envoi

1   Hitchens is a prolific journalist with, perhaps, an overactive nose for humbug and flummery. However, his exposé of Mother Theresa is consistently revealing. His account centers on her unsavory links with the Duvalier dynasty in Haiti and Union Carbide in India. He also highlights her extreme views on abortion and contraception. His account presents Mother Theresa as a more morally confused and reactionary figure than represented by the popular media and the Vatican view of late twentieth-century sainthood.

2   The medieval pilgrimages were blatantly organized around the notion of celebrity saints. An examination of the history of pilgrimages reveals an unexpectedly sophisticated network of ideological manipulation and cultural intermediaries which provided pilgrims with mementos and icons of featured saints.

REFERENCES

Arlacchi, P. (1986) *Mafia Business*. London: Verso.

Auster, A. (1999) Frank Sinatra: The Television Years, 1950–60. *Journal of Popular Film and Television* 28:4, 166–74.

Balliett, W. (1998) On Frank Sinatra 1915–1998. *New York Review of Books*, June 25, p. 13.

Blok, A. (1974) *The Mafia of a Sicilian Village, 1860–1960*. Oxford: Blackwell.

Boorstin, D. (1962) *The Image*. New York: Atheneum.

Clarke, D. (1995) *The Rise and Fall of Popular Music*. London: Penguin.

Clarke, D. (1997) *All or Nothing at All: A Life of Frank Sinatra*. Basingstoke: Macmillan.

Denton, S. and Morris, R. (2002) *The Money and the Power: The Making of Las Vegas and its Hold on America, 1947–2000*. London: Pimlico.

Evanier, D. (2002) *Making the Wiseguys Weep: The Jimmy Roselli Story*. London: Methuen.

Fowles, J. (1992) *Starstruck: Celebrity Performers and the American Public*. Washington, DC: Smithsonian Institution Press.

Freedland, M. (1997) *All the Way: A Biography of Frank Sinatra*. London: Orion.

Freud, S. (1910) *Leonardo da Vinci*. Harmondsworth: Penguin.

Friedwald, W. (1996) *Sinatra: The Song is You*. New York: Scribner.

Frith, S. (1998) *Performing Rites*. Oxford: Oxford University Press.

Giancana, S. and Giancana, C. (1992) *Double-Cross*. New York: Warner Books.

Granata, C. (1999) *Sessions with Sinatra*. Chicago: Cappella Books.

Gray, J. (2002) Fame is the Filthy Lucre of a Celebrity Economy. *Sunday Times News Review*, Oct. 28.

Hamill, P. (1998) *Why Sinatra Matters*. New York: Little, Brown.

Harvey, D. (1989) *The Condition of Postmodernity*. Oxford: Blackwell.

184

References

Herman, A. (2000) *Joseph McCarthy: Re-examining the Life and Legacy of America's Most Hated Senator*. New York: Free Press.

Hersh, S. (1998) *The Dark Side of Camelot*. London: HarperCollins.

Hess, H. (1998) *Mafia and Mafiosi*. London: Hurst.

Hitchens, C. (1995) *The Missionary Position: Mother Theresa in Theory and Practice*. London: Verso.

Hobsbawm, E. (1969) *Bandits*. New York: New Press.

Horowitz, P. (1967) *Understanding Toscanini*. New York: Knopf.

Hughes, D. (1974) *A History of European Music*. New York: McGraw Hill.

Humphrey, H. (1957) Sinatra is Calling his Own Signals Now. *New York Telegram*, Aug. 13.

Kelley, K. (1986) *My Way: The Unauthorized Biography of Frank Sinatra*. New York: Bantam Books.

Kempton, M. (1998) On Frank Sinatra 1915–1998. *New York Review of Books*, June 25, p. 13.

Kuntz, T. and Kuntz, P. (eds) (2000) *The Frank Sinatra Files*. New York: Three Rivers Press.

Lahr, J. (1998) *Sinatra: The Artist and the Man*. London: Phoenix.

Levinson, H. J. (1999) *Trumpet Blues: The Life of Harry James*. Oxford: Oxford University Press.

Levy, S. (1998) *Rat Pack Confidential*. New York: Doubleday.

Lowenthal, L. (1961) *Literature, Popular Culture and Society*. Palo Alto: Pacific Books.

Machiavelli, N. (1898) *The History of Florence ... The Prince*. London: George Bell.

Marcus, G. (2002) *The Manchurian Candidate*. London: British Film Institute.

Mead, G. H. (1934) *Mind, Self and Society*. Chicago: University of Chicago Press.

Meier, C. (1996) *Caesar*. London: Fontana.

Meyer G. (2002) Frank Sinatra: The Popular Front and an American Icon. *Science and Society* 56:3, 311–35.

Miller, J. (1999) *Almost Grown*. London: Arrow.

Mills, C. W. (1956) *The Power Elite*. New York: Oxford University Press.

Munn, M. (2001) *Sinatra: The Untold Story*. London: Robson.

O'Brien, D. (1998) *The Frank Sinatra Film Guide*. London: Batsford.

Petkov, S. and Mustazza, L. (eds) (1995) *The Frank Sinatra Reader*. New York: Oxford University Press.

Quirk, L. J. and Schoell, W. (1998) *The Rat Pack*. Dallas: Taylor.

References

Roberts, R. and Olson, J. (1995) *John Wayne, American*. New York: Free Press.

Rojek, C. (2001) *Celebrity*. London: Reaktion Books.

Schlesinger, A. (1978) *Robert Kennedy and his Times*. New York: Houghton Miffin.

Shaw, A. (1968) *Sinatra*. London: Hodder.

Simpson, C. (1988) *Blowback: America's Recruitment of Nazis and its Effect on the Cold War*. New York: Simon and Schuster.

Sinatra, F. (1947) As Sinatra Sees It. *New Republic*, Jan. 6, p. 45.

Sinatra, T. (with Coplon, J.) (2000) *My Father's Daughter: A Memoir*. New York: Simon and Schuster.

Taraborrelli, J. R. (1997) *Frank Sinatra: The Man and the Myth*. Edinburgh: Mainstream.

Thomson, D. (1994) *A Biographical Dictionary of Film*. London: Andre Deutsch.

Thomson, D. (2002) Rat Poison. *Independent*, Jan. 16, pp. 1 and 7.

Tönnies, F. (1887) *Gemeinschaft und Gesellschaft*. Trans. by Charles P. Loomis as *Community and Association*, London: Routledge and Kegan Paul, 1974.

Tosches, N. (1992) *Dino: Living High in the Dirty Business of Dreams*. London: Vintage.

Van Der Merwe, P. (1989) *Origins of the Popular Style*. Oxford: Oxford University Press.

Weiner, J. (1986) When Old Blue Eyes was Red: The Poignant Story of Frank Sinatra's Politics. *New Republic*, Mar. 31, pp. 21–3.

Weiner, J. (1991) *Professors, Politics and Pop*. London: Verso.

Williams, R. (2000) *Long Distance Call: Writings on Music*. London: Aurum Press.

Wills, G. (1988) *Reagan's America*. New York: Penguin.

Wills, G. (1997) *John Wayne's America: The Politics of Celebrity*. New York: Simon and Schuster.

Wills, G. (1999) *A Necessary Evil: A History of American Distrust of Government*. New York: Touchstone.

Witkin, R. (2003) *Adorno on Popular Culture*. London: Routledge.

Zehme, B. (1997) *The Way You Wear Your Hat: Frank Sinatra and the Lost Art of Livin'*. New York: HarperCollins.

INDEX

abortionist charge (Dolly
    Sinatra) 60
achieved Celebrity 45, 54, 101,
    102–6, 112, 116, 132, 161, 163,
    166–8
Adonis, J. 64
Adorno, T. 170–1, 172
Agnew, S. 4, 13, 52, 92, 93, 94
alcohol 97, 101, 113, 116, 138, 159
Aldrich, R. 144
Algonquin Round Table 121–2
Alta Italia 69–70
Amalgamated Clothing Workers
    Union 65
American dream 5
amorality 163, 171
Anastasia, A. 9, 63, 64, 65, 94
Anderson, R. (sheriff) 89, 95, 111
anomie 104
Arlaachi, p. 72, 75
Arnaz, D. 109
Astaire, F. 39
Auster, A. 157, 158

Bacall, L. 121, 122–4, 177
baldness (Sinatra's) 107
Balistieri, F. 79
Ball, L. 108
Balliet, F. 54

Basie, Count 2, 36, 54
Beatles 30, 127, 128
bel canto 171
Benny Goodman Band 39, 41
Billboard 14
Bishop, J. 17, 127, 159
Black Power movement 143
Blok, A. 71, 72, 74
Bogart, H. 119, 121, 122, 124, 127
Bono 5
Boorstin, D. 131, 165
Bruno, A. 80
business interests (Sinatra's with
    Mafia) 90, 91, 92, 94–5

Caan, S. 29, 30
Caesarism 30–2, 35, 46, 47, 54, 95,
    135, 161
Caesar's Palace 17
Cal-Neva Lodge 29, 50, 51, 53, 75,
    79, 88, 89, 95, 134
Castellamarerse wars 63–7, 168
Capitol Records 4, 14, 15, 24, 43,
    96, 130, 168
Capone, A. 9, 91
Carter, J. 4
Castro, F. 91
celebrity icons 1–2, 127–8
celetoid 131, 132, 165

Chaplin, C. 1
charity work (Sinatra's) 4, 21, 36,
  59, 106, 134, 176, 179
Cheshire, M. 141–2
CIA 59, 98, 178
civil rights movement 29
Clarke, D. 60, 61, 101, 111, 135, 146
Clinton, W. 101, 134, 175
Clooney, G. 5
Cobb, L. J. 35
Cohen, M. 79
Cold War 58, 75, 98, 137, 148
Coll, V. 'Mad Dog' 66
Columbia Records 3, 14, 15, 24,
  43, 96, 130, 168
Columbus Day Riot 18
communism 8, 10, 11, 12, 18, 20,
  49, 97, 151
concept album 43–4, 46
Connors, C. 145
consumer culture 15, 46, 47, 58,
  59, 118, 133, 137, 142, 148, 153,
  162, 167, 176
cool 30, 47, 55, 79, 107, 133, 139,
  146, 148, 149, 150, 152
Cooper, G. 109
Coppola, F. 70
Costello, F. 9, 63, 65, 69
counterculture 153–4, 159, 160
Crosby, B. 3. 14, 23, 36, 39, 40, 50,
  81, 97, 157

D'Amato, S. 76, 79, 80, 85, 89
Dagmar 13
Dark Ages (Sinatra's) 14, 18–22,
  79, 116–17, 127, 157, 167
Davis Jr, S. 17, 46, 77, 87, 88,
  117–8, 125–6, 138, 144, 159
De Carlo, G. 93, 94
Democratic Party 48, 52, 61, 76,
  102, 138, 174

Denton, S. 76, 146
Diana, Princess of Wales 19
Dickinson, A. 175
Douglas, K. 59
Dunaway, F. 153

Edison, T. 42
Eisenhower, D. 48, 133
escapism 137–9
Evanier, D. 16, 31, 80, 81
Evans, C. 103
Evans, G. 20, 23, 24, 25
Exner, J. Campbell 49, 84

Farrow, M. 105, 138
FBI 8, 12, 76, 82, 84, 85, 86–8, 90,
  91, 93, 94, 168, 179
Federalist Papers 151
feudalism 74
Fischetti, C. 78
Fischetti, J. 9, 90
Fischetti, R. 9
flexible accumulation 150
Fountainebleau Hotel, Miami 78,
  82
Fowles, J. 163
Franco, General 10
Freedland, M. 12, 52, 55, 89, 105,
  108
Freud, S. 45
Friedwald, W. 54, 113, 154, 173

Gambino, C. 63, 65, 78, 94, 95, 125
Garavante, B. 78
Garbo, G. 1, 116, 128
Gardner, A. 7, 14, 16, 23, 36, 44,
  48, 79, 89, 107, 108, 123, 126,
  135, 156, 169
Genovese, V. 65, 94
gesta (feats) 71, 73
Giancana, C. 84

Giancana, S. 4, 49, 50, 76, 80, 81–91, 95, 124
gift relations 68
Glitter, G. 20
Gotti, J. 65, 95
Granata, C. 96, 130, 161, 171
Grant, C. 128
Gray, J. 104

Hamill, P. 77, 171
Harry James Orchestra 17, 22, 41, 45, 135, 145
Harvey, D. 150
Hayworth, R. 10
Hefner, H. 149, 150
Heiftez, J. 37
Herman, A. 151
Hersh, S. 77
Hirohito, Emperor 99
Hitchens, C. 163
Hoboken 4 39, 40, 135
Holiday, B. 36
Hollywood Independent Citizens Committee of Arts, Sciences and Professions 10
Hollywood Ten 11
Hoover, E. 84
Hope, B. 53, 156
Hopper, E. 16
Hopper, H. 12
hot and cold media (McLuhan) 157
House of Un-American Activities Committee (HUAC) 11, 12, 49, 174, 178
hubris 3–4, 11
humility 20, 56
Humphrey, H. 157
Humphrey, Hubert 52, 85
hysteria 23

impotence (Sinatra's) 45
Internal Revenue Service 82
Italia Bassa 69

Jack Pack 110
Jackson, A. 48
Jackson, M. 19
Jacobs, G. 110
Jenkins, G. 15, 154, 155
Johnson, E. 34
Johnson, L. B. 52
Jolson, A. 3, 14, 23

Kelley, K. 60, 76, 106
Kempton, M. 17, 135, 169
Kennedy, J. 85–6
Kennedy, J. F. 4, 16, 21, 28–9, 47, 50, 52, 76, 80, 84, 85, 86, 88, 89, 106, 125, 126, 132, 175
Kennedy, P. 126
Kennedy, R. F. 29, 49, 85, 86, 87, 88, 89, 175
Kilgalen, D. 12

Lahr, J. 42, 60, 170
Lansky, M. 9, 66, 79, 90, 91, 147
Las Vegas 146–7
Lawford, P. 17, 77, 84, 87, 109–10, 126, 144, 159
legato style of singing 169
Lepke, L. 65, 66
Levinson, H. 2, 35
Levy, S. 119, 122, 126, 127, 174
Lincoln, A. 7
long-players 43
Lowenthal, D. 130
Luchese, T. 64, 66
Luciano, L. 9, 10, 63, 64, 65, 66, 68, 79, 80
Lugosi, B. 35
lust (female) 45

Machiavelli 179
MacLaine, S. 147
Mafia 8, 9, 10, 20, 27, 29, 53, 59,
    62–3, 63–7, 69, 72, 73–95, 99,
    107, 109, 125, 168, 175
Major Bowes Radio Show 40
Maltz. A. 11, 49, 50
Maranzano, S. 63, 64, 65, 66, 68
Marcus, G. 152
Martin, D. 17, 46, 77, 79, 87, 88,
    110, 124–5, 126, 136, 138, 140–1,
    144, 157, 158–9
Martin, D. Jr 140
Marx, B. 4, 101, 136, 146
masculinity 44, 58, 59, 62, 70–3,
    111, 118–19, 140, 177
Masseria, J. 63, 64
mastoiditis 8
May, B. 15
Mayer, L. B. 22, 126
McCarthy, J. 10, 18, 49, 98, 151,
    152
Mead, G. H. 115
Meier, C. 35
Mercer, M. 36
Metro-Goldwyn-Mayer
    (MGM) 3, 14, 22, 118, 153
Meyer, G. 11, 98
microphone 42, 43
Miller, J. 130
Miller, M. 13
Mills, C. W. 47
Minelli, L. 141
Monroe, M. 80, 88–9, 149
Moore, R. 145
Moretti, W. 9, 78, 79, 91, 125
Morris, R. 76, 147
Morrison, T. 89
Mortimer, L. 7, 11, 20, 34, 101
Munn, M. 88, 89, 90, 110
Mustazza, L. 171

narcissism 35, 36, 112–5, 116, 133,
    172, 177
Nevada Gaming Control
    Board 17, 29, 50, 52, 53, 176
New Deal 12
Niven, D. 121
Nixon, R. 4, 13, 17, 48, 52, 93, 94,
    132

Olson, J. 99
omerta 25, 71, 72, 88, 92

Paramount Theater (New
    York) 18
Parker, Colonel Tom 57
Parsons, L. 12, 123
parvenu status 100, 102, 167, 173
Patriarca, R. 91–2
patriotism 7, 26, 27, 28, 33, 34, 96,
    97, 98, 142, 152
Peck, G. 10, 53, 145
Petkov, S. 171
Playboy 20, 21, 149–51, 170, 172
police 62, 111
power 51, 54, 56, 58, 77, 89, 95, 98,
    101, 102, 134, 160, 174–9
Presley, E. 30–1, 57, 108, 128, 130,
    139, 153, 157
Profaci, J. 63, 64
Prohibition 62, 75, 77
Provine, D. 108
Prowse, J. 107–8, 177
public face (of celebrity) 1, 6, 45,
    53, 56, 58, 105, 113, 115–17, 136,
    163

Quirk, L. J. 89, 109, 110, 118, 119,
    122, 176

racism 61, 63, 67, 70, 71, 96, 138,
    143

radio 39, 170
Rancho Mirage 84, 145–6
Rat Pack 5–6, 17–18, 21, 26, 29, 39, 45, 47, 68, 88, 96, 118–20, 121–60
RCA Records 14
Reagan, N. 13, 52, 53, 174
Reagan, R. 13, 16, 51–3, 132, 133, 134, 175, 176
reality TV 132
Red Menace 10
Reles, A. 67
religion 113, 164–5
Reprise Records 21, 30, 142–3, 168
Republican Party 13, 52, 102, 134, 138, 174
Rich, B. 35, 41
Riddle, N. 15
Roberts, R. 99
Rockwell, N. 109
Rolling Stones 30, 128
Roosevelt, F. 12, 48, 56
Roselli, J. 16, 77, 80, 81, 95
Rudin, M. 4

Sacco, N. 9
Sacks, M. 24
Saint Valentine's Day Massacre 81
Sands Hotel 51, 53, 75, 82, 88, 90, 95, 105, 146
Sanicola, H. 79
Schlesinger, A. 84, 175
Schoell, W. 89, 109, 110, 118, 119, 122, 176
Senate Select Committee on Crime 92, 175
sexual life (of Sinatra) 2, 23, 24, 31, 45, 130, 167, 176
Shaw, A. 19, 36, 42, 63, 71, 81, 110, 148, 172

Sicily 25, 51, 68, 69, 72, 74, 103, 177
Siegel, B. 64, 79, 91, 147
Silvers, P. 100
Simpson, C. 98
Simpson, O. J. 20
Sinatra, D. 25, 38, 60–1, 68, 69, 126, 134
Sinatra, F. Jr 106
Sinatra, Nancy (wife) 23, 24, 78
Sinatra, Nancy (daughter) 106
Sinatra, T. 16, 33, 55, 76, 95, 97, 101, 115, 129, 168, 178
social bandits 74
soldierly air (of Sinatra) 96–7, 99, 101, 178
Stompanato, J. 79
Stop Communism Committee 98
Stordahl, A. 15
suicide attempts (Sinatra's) 24
Sun City 54

tabloid press 2
Taraborrelli, J. R. 17, 45, 54, 56, 60, 101, 110–11
Tarantino, J. 79
Tarantino, Q. 5
Teamsters Central State Pension Fund 85
television 155–7
Tenney, J. B. 10
Thomson, D. 101
tipping 67, 115
Tommy Dorsey Band 17, 22, 23, 37, 39, 41, 42, 45, 69, 106, 135, 145, 168
Tönnies, F. 131
Tosches, N. 29, 140–1, 159
Trafficante, S. 9, 78
Tunney, J. 92, 175

Index

United Services Organization 100
uomo d'onore 50, 71, 177
uomo di rispetto 48, 50, 51, 53, 56,
57, 72, 174, 177

Valentino, R. 23
Vallee, R. 23, 39, 40
Van Heusen, J. 17, 24, 30, 109,
115, 121
Vanzetti, B. 9
vaudeville 38–9, 139, 141
Villa Venice (Chicago) 88
violence (of Sinatra) 34–5, 51, 91,
105, 108, 109–11, 141, 170–1
vocal art (of Sinatra) 32–3, 36, 37,
42, 55, 161, 169, 170–1
Volstead Act 62

vote-rigging (West Viriginia
Primary) 84–5
vulnerability 112, 123, 135, 136

Wallach, E. 70
Warner Brothers 142–3
Watergate 94
Wayne, J. 34, 99
Weiner, J. 11, 12, 49, 138, 142
Williams, R. 22
Williams, Robbie 5, 19
Willis, G. 132, 143, 144
Winchell, W. 8
Witkin, R. 162, 170, 172
Women's Press Club 22

Zehme, B. 104, 115, 117, 147, 148